REBUILDING **MANCHESTER**

REBUILDING **MANCHESTER**

Euan Kellie

◄ Aerial view of Manchester city centre with Piccadilly
Station and Piccadilly Place at the foot of the image,
February 2010.
Argent Estates Limited

MANCHESTER CITY CENTRE 2010

- Victoria
- Northern Quarter
- Piccadilly Gateway
- Eastern Gateway
- Oxford Road Corridor
- Southern Gateway
- Castlefield
- Chapel Street, Salford
- Retail Core
- The Village
- China Town
- Central Business District
- Petersfield
- Spinningfields

ACKNOWLEDGEMENTS

Like many of the stories that follow, it has only been possible to deliver the book as a result of partnerships and support (and excessive amounts of coffee, varying greatly in quality).

First and foremost, it would simply not have been possible to complete (or start) the book without the support of my parents, George and Elaine. Nor would it have gone anywhere without my wonderful girlfriend Kelly. Thanks also to my sister, Morag, who was always there to offer support when I needed it. This book is, therefore, dedicated to them. I wouldn't (couldn't) have done it without them.

EXTENDED THANKS GO TO THE FOLLOWING:

Photographer Aidan O'Rourke, whose wonderful generosity led to the inclusion of his fantastic photographs in this book (and on the front cover). Without these images the book would not be what it is (see www.aidan.co.uk for more).

Two former city council officers: Dave Robinson, who expertly enabled me to see the stories and themes when I couldn't see the wood for the trees; and Warren Marshall, blessed with a memory of projects akin to that of a black-box recorder.

My good friend David Holman, who gave up his time on a number of occasions to meet up and discuss the text.

Jesse Davison-Hulme and Alex Pritchett who undertook some sterling research work during the early days of the project.

All those at DB Publishing, who chose to support the venture. Their positive, pro-active approach throughout the whole process really kept me going.

And finally, all of the many, many people who took time out from their busy schedules to kindly meet me, provide me with photographs and documents, discuss the concept and share their ideas (thanks also to the various PAs who played a crucial role in arranging these meetings and collating background material).

First published in Great Britain in 2010 by The Derby Books Publishing Company Limited Breedon House, 3 The Parker Centre, Derby, DE21 4SZ.

ISBN 978-1-85983-786-3
Printed and bound by Progress Press, Malta.

Cover photograph © Aidan O'Rourke - www.aidan.co.uk

CONTENTS

REBUILDING MANCHESTER

This book was initially inspired by Manchester's response to the catastrophic impact of the UK's largest mainland bomb since World War Two, detonated in the heart of the city centre at 11.17am on Saturday 15 June 1996.

But **Rebuilding Manchester** is not just about the replacement of bomb-damaged buildings. The response to the events of 15 June 1996 were part of a much bigger story, rebuilding the whole notion of Manchester as a thriving, vibrant, creative city following years of post-war economic decline.

I have been fortunate to witness first hand the radical re-birth of Manchester as one of Europe's great cities. It has regained its identity as a place of leadership and exciting new ideas. It is a place where people want to be - where people **choose** to be.

This story is truly inspirational.

FOREWORD

Throughout this book you are taken on a historic and candid journey of Manchester's birth and rebirth. Each turn of the page wonderfully illustrates the ever-changing face of the city streets, from its days of innovation and industry during Victorian England to the ambitious home and workplace it is today.

Manchester was the cradle of the Industrial Revolution, ushering in the era of modernity which turned the world into a global village. From the first railway station, to the first scheduled airline service, first computer and first professional Football League, Manchester has always been at the forefront of invention and has helped make the world a smaller place.

It has encountered many defining moments in its history, and it has been my privilege during a short time to play a small role in shaping this great city.

A defining moment, one might say, occurred on 15 June 1996 when a terrorist attack by the IRA brought devastation both physically and emotionally to the city, its residents and myself as a fellow Mancunian. Upon reading this book and seeing the pictures again, I was reminded not only of the horrific events of that fateful morning and the awful devastation that rocked Manchester but also the sense of relief that there was no loss of life, which was miraculous. Once the initial shock had surpassed, our city was left with choices within the aftermath that had devastated the fabric of our city centre.

In the days, weeks, months and now years since the attack Manchester has been rebuilding and reinventing itself. The devastation inflicted on that day opened a door of opportunity that saw Manchester re-evaluate and ultimately start again and was the catalyst that continues in motion today to push the city forward. This journey has been one of epic proportions – a vast city-wide evolution not seen, I feel, since the days Manchester was the beating heart at the centre of the Industrial Revolution.

For me, Manchester is not just a city that looks to the past, it is a creative, forward-looking city. The people here have an industrious work ethic and thirst for innovation which creates a unique opportunity. The private businesses in partnership with ourselves and other public bodies, as well as the general communities and neighbourhoods across the city, have all contributed greatly in shaping and growing this city.

Manchester describes itself as the original modern city – a city which celebrates the rich texture of its glorious past while thriving on being at the forefront of the world.

We are now in a new revolution of sorts and one that I am honoured and proud to be a part of, as it has brought with it many triumphs and achievements, including the Commonwealth Games in 2002 – the largest multi-sport event ever hosted in the UK to date – and the opening in 2007 of one of the UK's tallest buildings, the now iconic Manchester Beetham Tower.

However, you could say Manchester's real success that resulted from rebuilding the heart of the city was that it ensured the centre could be the lifeblood for a wider economic geography that extends beyond boundaries. What has been achieved in these past 15 or so years provides a platform for even greater, sustainable growth going forward – successful cities can never stand still, and Manchester needs to keep creating the next page.

It is a great…and never-ending story.

Sir Howard Bernstein

Chief Executive
Manchester City Council

'Manchester is the envy of any other urban centre in Europe, a modern metropolis that has embraced 21st century style and technology like no other in Britain.'

— Lonely Planet Guide, 2007

INTRODUCTION

So, what is this book? Without doubt it is a story.

Primarily it seeks to capture and explain how Manchester city centre has changed (and expanded) significantly following the UK's largest mainland bomb since World War Two, which was detonated on 15 June 1996. It is, however, impossible and unjust to isolate this incident and associated rebuilding and investment from the years of effort, energy and repositioning that came before. This process of evolution meant that Manchester City Council could not have been better placed to deal positively and pro-actively with the devastation. Seamlessly, the response to the bomb was woven into the fabric of the city, into its existing objectives and ambitions. And it did not stop there. In the years that followed the reconstruction of the bomb core, the city centre continued to change and expand at a sensational rate.

Throughout the book, several themes and processes appear time and time again: partnership, investment, commitment, persistence, commerciality, creativity, dedication, quality (across a series of levels) and deliverability. Another theme is success: job creation, financial growth, attracting tourists and winning awards (architecture in particular). In conjunction, the city council has never lost the thirst and hunger to maintain Manchester's position as the regional capital of the North West; England's second city.

The story about Manchester city centre is not just about events and processes. It is about people. The axis of Sir Howard Bernstein and Sir Richard Leese at the city council. The drive of property entrepreneurs such as Carol Ainscow, Jim Ramsbottom, Peter Dalton, Nick Johnson and Tom Bloxham MBE. The vision and creativity of Manchester's architects: Ian Simpson and Rachel Haugh, Roger Stephenson OBE and Stephen Hodder MBE, to name but a few. The drive and focus of developers and investors such as Ask, Argent, Allied London and Bruntwood. The hundreds of people who have worked with, and on behalf of, these individuals, companies and organisations. And, of course, the tens of

The story is also one of risk: Manchester City Council supporting and backing ventures and initiatives that may not have worked in other cities. Swimming pools inside the Manchester Evening News Arena, tall buildings, on paper, peppered across the city centre – rising in places up to 60 storeys, Usain Bolt sprinting up Deansgate on a wet Sunday afternoon. The sheer audacity of not one but two Olympic bids. And then the Commonwealth Games!

It has not been plain sailing, though, and there have been setbacks and fresh challenges: the failed bid to secure planning permission for the Free Trade Hall in 1998, the congestion charge rejected by the public 10 years later, ongoing problems with the elegant London Road Fire Station, the difficulties with the Great Northern Warehouse, the challenge of providing public open space that works, schemes that have not been built, schemes that have been part-built and now lie derelict. And, of course, the bomb. What is clear, though, is that Manchester city centre is a real success. It has become an exemplar, a model; a place to live, shop, relax and do business.

This book seeks to rewind, play, and then fast forward, in the process celebrating all that is has been achieved in Manchester city centre. Could this book, therefore, be regarded as a manual for city centre regeneration? Quite possibly.

Euan Kellie
May 2010

'What Manchester does today, the rest of the world does tomorrow.'

— Benjamin Disraeli

WELCOME TO MANCHESTER

'Man – ches - ter [man-ches-ter, -chuh-ster] – noun
1. a city in NW England: connected with the Mersey estuary by a ship canal (35.5 miles [57km] long).'
– Taken from Dictionary.com

LET THE STORY BEGIN. WHERE AND WHAT IS MANCHESTER?

Manchester is a city. To provide a geographical context, the city is 40 miles (65km) to the east of Liverpool, 220 miles (355km) south of Edinburgh and Glasgow and 200 miles (320km) north west of London. Regionally, it lies within the conurbation of Greater Manchester, one of the United Kingdom's largest metropolitan areas, which includes towns such as Bolton, Bury, Oldham, Rochdale, Salford, Stockport, Trafford and Wigan. When counted in 2007 the city had a population of approximately 458,000 people. It is important to understand the regional significance of the city: 11.5 million people live within a 50-mile (80km) radius. Economically, Greater Manchester has a significant labour pool and a strong single economy – estimated to be worth £50 billion.

What do people tend to associate with Manchester when they hear the name? Industry? Probably. Football? Definitely. Music? No question. While this is all true, there is also quite an inspirational archive of entrepreneurship, resilience, determination and a 'can-do' attitude.

The main focus of the book is Manchester city centre, with the 'study area' framed by the Mancunian Way to the east and south, Great Ancoats Street to the north and the River Irwell to the west (also known as the Manchester and Salford Inner Relief Route). Due to the expanding nature of the city centre, however, it cannot be considered in isolation from its surroundings; consequently, reference is made to a number of projects and initiatives on the border and immediately outside this area.

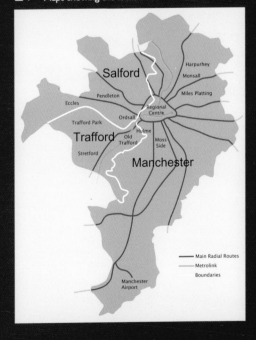

▲▼ Maps showing the location of Manchester.

REBUILDING **MANCHESTER**

▶ Map of Manchester, 1650.

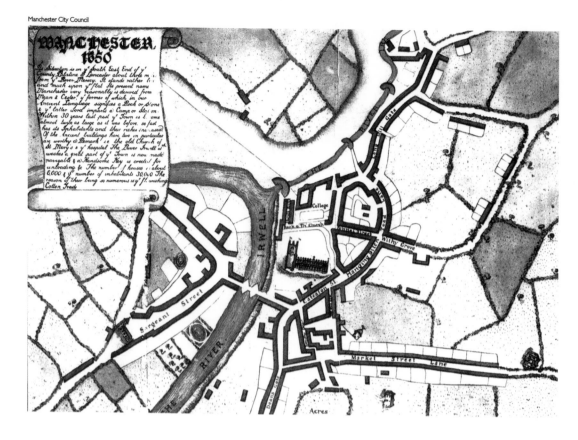

As a first step, it seems appropriate and relevant to set the scene by introducing Manchester's economic history and physical evolution over recent centuries. It is quite a story. What will, hopefully, be apparent throughout the book is that many of the visions and principles that were adopted way back in the 18th century are still valid today.

MANCHESTER'S EVOLUTION

Manchester's economic history and physical evolution is truly fascinating. It was little more than a small town in 1750, yet the transformation began in 1761 when the Bridgewater Canal opened. This was a project commissioned by the Duke of Bridgewater, Francis Egerton, to bring cheap coal to Manchester from the mines in Worsley, Salford. By the end of the 18th century Manchester had established itself as the centre of the cotton industry in Lancashire, and it quickly moved from the seventh most populated town in the United Kingdom to the third. The hunger and thirst for trade and commerce led to the Liverpool railway being constructed in 1829, which in turn initiated even greater growth in transport and the exchange of goods.

In 1835 it became the first industrial city centre in the world. Manchester, at this time, was helping to shape and mould the newly emerging global economy. It seemed only right that in 1851 Manchester was granted 'city' status. During this remarkable rise Manchester was, without doubt, the regional heart of the North West and the leading banking,

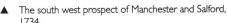

commercial and transportation centre outside London. The population grew dramatically, and by 1851 over 455,000 people were living in the city. Manchester's city fathers, however, were not prepared to rest on their laurels. Seeking further economic growth, the Manchester Ship Canal, which would give the city direct access to the sea for its imports and its exports of manufactured goods (and bypass Liverpool for tax reasons), was constructed between 1887 and 1894. This remarkable project cost approximately £15 million (estimated to be more than £1 billion in 2010) and was,

▲ The south west prospect of Manchester and Salford, 1734.

◄ An early print of Liverpool Road Station and Water Street Bridge, 1830.

REBUILDING **MANCHESTER**

▶ Union Street Mill, Ancoats, 1835.

at the time, the largest navigation canal in the world. With the incorporation of the canal, Manchester also became the third-largest port in the country – quite perverse, bearing in mind it is approximately 30 miles (50km) from the Irish Sea.

▼ Construction of the Manchester Ship Canal, 1890.

Unsurprisingly, the city was viewed by many as an inspiration – a real trailblazer. Individuals of considerable importance such as Alexis de Tocqueville (a French political thinker and historian best known for his text *Democracy in America*), Charles Dickens, Fredrick Engels and Karl Marx all visited Manchester between 1835 and 1880 to learn more. Marx in particular was captivated and paid 24 separate visits to the city during this period (it was at Chetham's Library where Marx and Engels wrote and researched the book *Das Kapital*). It was not all good, though; Engels was shocked by the poverty in the city, which led to him writing the book *Condition of the Working Class in England*, published in 1844.

Notwithstanding, at the time it seemed to be the place where anything could happen. The then Prime Minister Benjamin Disraeli famously once remarked:

'What Manchester does today, the rest of the world does tomorrow.'

The city centre was the hub of this activity, with a landscape dominated by mills, warehouses, canals and railways. It became a unique product of this period of phenomenal economic growth, mirrored by the wealth of Victorian buildings that started to appear on the skyline – something that was not missed by *Builder* magazine in the 1870s, which described Manchester as being architecturally finer than London.

▼ View of the city centre from the Town Hall, 1934.

Manchester Archives and Local Studies

REBUILDING **MANCHESTER**

▲ Midland Hotel.

▲ St George's House (former YMCA), Peter Street.

▼ Midland Bank, King Street.

As the city rolled into the 20th century, its veritable economic success and prosperity continued to deliver some wonderful pieces of architecture. Such fine buildings included Trubshaw's Midland Hotel (1903); St George's House (former YMCA) on Peter Street (1907–11); the Midland Bank on King Street (1929); the Town Hall Extension (completed over a four-year period between 1934–38); Kendal Milne on Deansgate (1939); and the Daily Express Building on Great Ancoats Street (1939). These really were buildings fit for a city that was going places.

In the years leading up to World War Two, Manchester's population had peaked at approximately 766,300, and the city was holding up well economically. There were, however, some worrying signs on the horizon. World War Two had had a profound effect by cutting off the export of British-made cloth, and over the next three decades this market collapsed. It was only a matter of time before Manchester would start to suffer.

▼ Town Hall extension under construction, 1935.

Manchester Archives and Local Studies

© Aidan O'Rourke - www.aidan.co.uk

▲ Kendals department store, Deansgate.

◀ The former Daily Express Building, on the corner of Great Ancoats Street and Lever Street.

▶ The front cover of the City of Manchester Plan 1945.

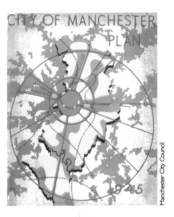

▼ Royal Exchange bomb damage, 1940.

REBUILDING AFTER THE BLITZ

Between 1939 and 1945 Manchester was hit hard. It was during this period that the city's landscape altered more dramatically than at any other time in its history. On 22 December 1940 many of the city's fine Victorian buildings were hit in a 48-hour offensive by the German Luftwaffe, including the Free Trade Hall – considered by many as a symbol of the city's greatness – the Royal Exchange, Manchester Cathedral and Piccadilly Gardens.

In the aftermath, the city, just like many other cities in the United Kingdom that were affected by the Blitz, like Coventry and Southampton, needed major planning and investment. Manchester City Council began to plan the city's future.

The 1945 'City of Manchester Plan' was prepared under wartime conditions for the council by the then City Surveyor and Engineer Roland Nicholas. Comprising wonderfully titled chapters such as 'learning, medicine and the arts' and the 'abolition of smoke', it was a document prepared for the whole city – which of course, included the bomb-damaged city centre. It sought to provide a framework for Manchester's future in terms of architecture, public realm and preferred land uses.

▶ Miller Street during the Blitz, 1940.

Manchester Archives and Local Studies

On 22 December 1940 many of the city's fine Victorian buildings were hit in a 48-hour offensive by the German Luftwaffe

By as early as the second paragraph the direction of the document, and Manchester's planned future, was clear:

'Most of Manchester has been built or rebuilt in the last half-century; but because the process went on unplanned, the city we live in is not a great improvement on the Manchester of 50 years ago. Individual buildings have changed, but congestion, dirt and ugliness remain.'

Chapter 18 was devoted to 'The City Centre'. Nicholas was not at all impressed with the 'face of Manchester' and its composition of buildings:

'What is it like, then, this central core which means so much to the city, to the region, to the country and to the world? Climb a tall building and what do you see – assuming that the day is fine? Looking eastward across the city centre, our frontispiece presents a picture typical of the British industrial scene: on the skyline a few new office buildings, gleaming white and clean against a smoke-pall laden with the soot that will soon darken them to the sombre hue of their less recent neighbours, and eventually to the dead black of the Town Hall tower; in the foreground, a jumble of derelict warehouses and narrow alleys – a dingy squalor that has long out-lived its time.'

The vision for the city centre was bold to say the least. It effectively proposed the demolition of almost all city-centre buildings, including the Town Hall, while providing grand areas of public open space.

Manchester Archives and Local Studies

◀ Longridge House, Corporation Street, 1966.

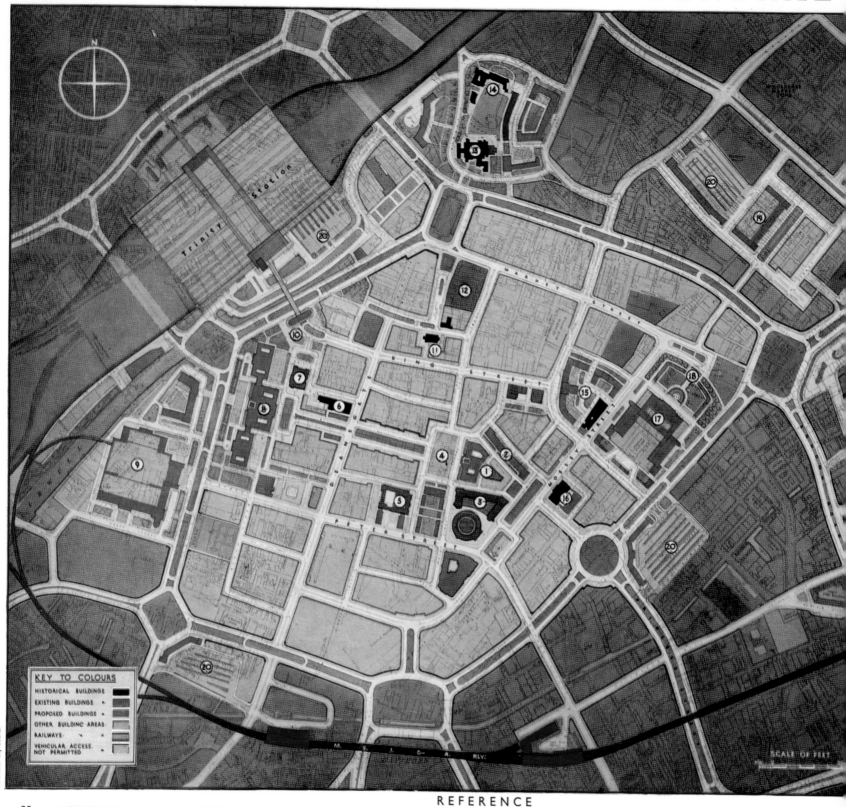

REFERENCE

1. TOWN HALL	4. ALBERT SQUARE	7. MASONIC TEMPLE	10. TRINITY STATION ANNEXE	13. CATHEDRAL	16. ART GALLERY	19.
2. PROPOSED EXTENSION	5. POLICE HEADQUARTERS	8. COURTS OF LAW	11. SAINT ANN'S CHURCH	14. CHETHAM'S HOSPITAL	17. AMUSEMENT CENTRE	20.
3. EXISTING EXTENSION	6. RYLANDS LIBRARY	9. EXHIBITION HALL	12. ROYAL EXCHANGE	15. COMMERCIAL CENTRE	18. PICCADILLY GARDENS	

KEY TO COLOURS

HISTORICAL BUILDINGS
EXISTING BUILDINGS
PROPOSED BUILDINGS
OTHER BUILDING AREAS
RAILWAYS
VEHICULAR ACCESS NOT PERMITTED

SCALE OF FEET

Manchester was not the only place where such grand visions were penned. In 1944 the 'Greater London Plan' was published. Prepared by respected town planner Sir Patrick Abercrombie, the vision was to move a million and a half people from London to new towns, with the goal of controlling sprawl. The objective for London and Manchester, along with many other cities, was to remove much of the Victorian past, with the axiom of 'if we can build better, we can live better'. Perhaps thankfully, few of Nicholas' grandiose visions actually came to fruition in Manchester city centre.

In the immediate post-war years Manchester city centre saw very few new buildings – a constraint mainly imposed by the extent of the damage caused by World War Two, along with fiscal constraints at the national level. It was not until the tail-end of the 1950s

▲   Granada TV offices.

when new buildings began to appear, one of the first being the office building Longridge House, located on the junction of Corporation Street and Cannon Street in the heart of the city centre. Designed by architects Harry S. Fairhurst and Son, the seven-storey building was the first to be completed after the war on a re-planned city-centre site. The building would have a significant role to play less than 40 years after its completion, which will be explained later in the book.

Another landmark building, also of strategic and symbolic importance, that arrived during this time was that of Granada House, designed by Ralph Tubbs for Granada Television Centre. Completed in 1962 and built on bomb-cleared land adjacent to the River Irwell, it was the outcome of a decision made by Granada to have their main control base in the centre of Manchester. It was a radical decision, as they became the first British television company to create facilities purpose-built for television production. The construction also 'beat' the BBC Television Centre in London by four years. So, even though it was a century after the Industrial Revolution, Manchester still had the desire to achieve and to be a leader.

The 1960s was a period of significant change in the city centre, particularly in terms of new buildings and their architectural form. As money steadily became available and confidence returned, the cityscape pattern began to change and gradually the areas damaged by the war were cleared and rebuilt.

◄   Proposed map of Manchester city centre, taken from the City of Manchester Plan 1945.

REBUILDING **MANCHESTER**

▲ North Tower.

▼ Portland Tower.

Such completed developments which, without doubt, changed the character and grain of Manchester city centre had a common theme: height. They included:

Building	Location	Height	Completion
The Co-operative Insurance Society (CIS) Tower	Miller Street	25 storeys	1962
St Andrew's House (now known as Portland Tower)	Portland Street	22 storeys	1962
Sunley Tower (now known as City Tower)	Piccadilly Plaza	29 storeys	1965
Highland House (now known as North Tower)	Victoria Bridge Street	23 storeys	1966

▲ CIS Tower.

▼ City Tower and Piccadilly Plaza under construction, 1960.

© Euan Kellie

◀ Crown Court, Spinningfields.

At the time, buildings such as these were seen as 'futuristic', commercial and significantly different to the grimy residue of the Victorian past. A number of these new developments were built without a tenant in place (known as speculative development), which meant that, until a business chose to 'take up' floorspace, the buildings would remain vacant and devoid of activity.

As new developments appeared on the skyline, plan-making continued in Manchester. The 1945 Plan was followed by the 1961 'Development Plan' prepared by Manchester City Council. Less radical, and much shorter, the document was still intent on bringing significant change to Manchester. The focus this time, however, was on dramatic highway improvements and the substantial rebuilding of nine war-damaged areas in the city centre: Strangeways, Market Place, Water Street (including the Courts of Law – one of the few visions from the 1945 Plan that was built), Swan Street, Shudehill, Piccadilly, Portland Street, Oxford Street and Faulkner Street.

Six years later, in 1967 Manchester City Council published the 'City Centre Map'. This was a policy document that followed on from the 1945 Plan which addressed transport, housing, shopping and commercial activity. The primary objective was to reinforce Manchester's central role within the conurbation and region. The Plan also, for the first time, promoted housing in the city centre to combat the effect of suburbanisation which had led to a dispersal of the city-centre population. The city council realised that this concept could provide positive linkages with the rest of the city centre by reducing traffic created by people travelling to work. It would also bring life back into the centre at all hours.

REBUILDING **MANCHESTER**

▲ London Road Station Warehouse, Ducie Street, 1966.

▼ Derelict Central Station following closure in 1969, with the Town Hall in the background.

The other core aspirations outlined in the plan were to provide a new road network that took extraneous traffic around, as opposed to through, the centre and thereby improving necessary access to the centre and its facilities. It would also allow environmental improvement while providing good-quality retail. In other words, the pedestrian experience would be improved. The sum of these parts would be a city that stood out from other towns and cities – a place where people would want (and choose) to be. Despite these visions and new buildings, Manchester was entering particularly dark economic times – not helped by the effects of national economic recession and changes in the world economy.

ECONOMIC COLLAPSE

The 1970s were, economically, undoubtedly a difficult decade for Manchester. Employment in industry and warehousing continued to fall sharply (by almost 50 per cent) with the decline of the textiles, clothing and engineering sectors. This was compounded by the loss of 30,000 manual manufacturing jobs between 1962 and 1972 – one third of the total employment at the time. Portions of the city centre gradually became dominated and characterised by empty factories and warehouses as, one by one, major businesses either became insolvent or relocated elsewhere. The railway stations that symbolised trade and growth were also hit by what became known as 'The Beeching Axe'. The government report prepared by Dr Richard Beeching in 1963 proposed that of Britain's 18,000 miles (3,000km) of railway, 6,000 miles (9,600km) of mostly rural branch and cross-country lines should close. The impact of the report in Manchester city centre was captured by the closure of the Great Northern Warehouse in 1963 and Manchester Central station and Exchange station in 1969.

The deep and debilitating recession of the early 1980s continued to push the city towards diversification as manufacturing and production were no longer the dominant sectors in the local economy. Instead there was a growth in the service sector, in particular within health and education. Alarmingly, the city's population was falling dramatically. In 1971 it was down to 543,859. Ten years later it had slumped further to 449,200 – almost half the figure it had been just before World War Two. The problems in Manchester continued outside the city centre in July 1981 with the Moss Side riots, the ultimate symbol of unrest.

Plan making continued and the city council tried to put these negative effects in reverse. The 1984 'City Centre Local Plan' sought to cure what was becoming, in economic terms, an unhealthy city. It stated:

'Maintaining and enhancing the range of activities in the City Centre will be the main aim of the Local Plan. The goal is a City Centre that is economically sound; respects its own history; is easy to get to; is a pleasant and safe place in which to move around once there, and has the wide variety of activities and land uses that is generally difficult to generate but which is the key characteristic of a major Regional Centre.'

It was during this decade that Manchester steadily began to reinvent and reposition itself. The Conservatives won the General Election in 1979, 1983 and 1987 and introduced a new form of urban regeneration, built around the social, economic and physical development of cities that had hit troubled times. This provided the perfect backdrop to Manchester's new approach.

THE NEW *MODUS OPERANDI*

Outlined beautifully by commentators Jamie Peck and Kevin Ward in their book *City of Revolution*, the city council slowly but surely began to work both pragmatically and imaginatively with the private sector and the Government:

'"Shorthand" forms of communication between members of the city's newly empowered elite would begin to displace the formal decision-making structures of council committees; cappuccinos and designer cakes at meetings in café bars replaced luke-warm tea and biscuits at the Town Hall.'

With the direction of new City Council Leader Graham Stringer, who had taken up his post in 1984, Manchester City Council suddenly had a clear economic strategy in place with a drive towards reversing the economic decline and also working pro-actively with the private sector, a concept previously frowned upon during the centralisation of the post-war Labour governments. This was perfectly symbolised by the change in the city council's slogan from 'Defending Jobs, Improving Services' (1985) to 'Making It Happen' (1990). A spirit that, in a sense, forms the spine of this story.

It is difficult to pin down one particular event that marked this new *modus operandi*, but one great example of the emerging entrepreneurial attitude is that of the 'Phoenix Initiative', launched in 1986. This was a coalition of major private sector companies, including building societies, which followed the American urban regeneration partnership model that had been successfully utilised in the early 1980s in cities such as Baltimore, Boston, Minneapolis and Pittsburgh. It recognised the value of public and private sectors working in partnership. As outlined by author Michael Carley in his 1990 text *Housing and Neighbourhood Renewal - Britain's New Urban Challenge*, this process broke down the barriers and enabled all parties to work together so that a cohesive vision could be achieved.

In Manchester the initiative, which was launched in 1987, was an amalgam of individuals from the public and private sector. It sought to raise financial investment from both the public purse and private sources so that derelict land

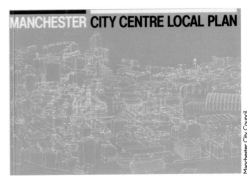

▲ The front cover of the Manchester City Centre Local Plan 1984.

▲ Manchester City Council logo, 1985.

▼ Manchester City Council logo, 1990.

REBUILDING **MANCHESTER**

▶ Land-use map of the city centre, 1985.

Predominantly Residential

Shops, Offices and Other Commercial

Community Facilities

Industry and Transport

Open Space

Vacant Land

Manchester City Council

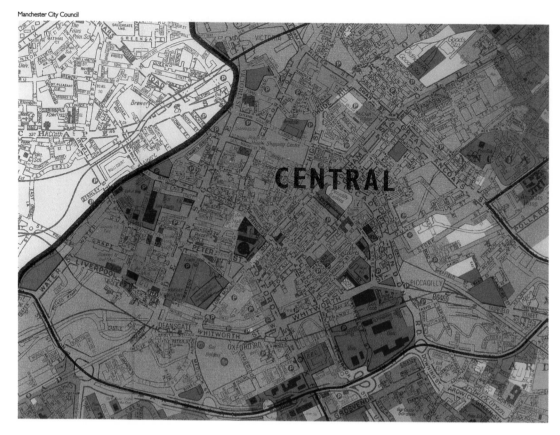

CENTRAL

adjacent to the Rochdale Canal basin, running from east to west across the city along Whitworth Street and characterised by large and old vacant warehouses, a symbol of the economic decline, could be regenerated.

The change in direction and the introduction of public-private partnerships was strengthened further by the creation of the Central Manchester Development Corporation (CMDC) in 1988. By this time the economic balance in Greater Manchester was starting to change. During the period of 1981 to 1987 those employed in manufacturing continued to fall, this time from 345,600 to 292,200, although much of the city centre was, in land use terms, dominated by industry and transport. Those employed in banking and finance grew by 18,400 (a 24 per cent increase), and in addition employment in public administration grew by 31,000. Manchester was starting to change.

Urban Development Corporations

Urban Development Corporations (UDCs) were a principal flagship of urban policy in the 1980s. Between 1981 and 1993 12 UDCs were established in England, of which Manchester was one. The concept, driven by national government, was to introduce a faster and more commercially sensitive approach to urban regeneration. Their remits emphasised the physical aspects of regeneration within designated Urban Development Areas (UDAs). They were given a range of statutory powers: to acquire, improve, service and dispose of land; to assist environmental improvements; and to encourage the restoration of existing buildings.

Once again, Manchester was at the front of the queue, the CMDC being the country's first such corporation to be orientated around a city centre (others were focused around docks such as London Docklands and Plymouth). In an interview with the *Estates Gazette* on 4 July 1992, Chief Executive of the Corporation, John Glester, explained why Manchester had been selected:

'The Government recognised that Manchester city centre had the capacity to become more than a nine-to-five workplace.'

The responsibility of the CMDC was sizeable, comprising 500 acres of land and 8.5 miles (13.5km) of waterways, extending from Pomona Docks at Salford Quays to the west and extending east to Great Ancoats Street. The area was characterised by large numbers of commercial businesses, listed buildings and conservation areas and portions of derelict and disused land. With a total budget of £101 million, the CMDC aimed to extend the mix of city-centre functions into the area (many of which at this time were constrained to the central business district, principally around Fountain Street and Mosley Street) and to diversify the mix of uses. The goal of attracting residents back to the city centre, introduced in the 1967 City Centre Map, also accelerated with a generous mix of new-build and the refurbishment of many of the city's warehouses. The CMDC went on to play a leading role in the regeneration of Castlefield where it helped to create a vibrant canal-basin complex of leisure and cultural industries.

The relationship between the city council and the CMDC was strong, with both playing an active role in the regeneration and rebranding of the city. This partnership approach was strengthened by City Council Leader Graham Stringer taking up a position on the CMDC Board.

The CMDC was a success. A notable achievement, among many, was the completion of the Bridgewater Hall. Designed by architects Renton Howard Wood Levin (RHWL), appointed following an architectural competition held in 1989, construction of the building commenced on 22 March 1993 and would deliver an international concert venue which would also be the home for three resident orchestras: the Hallé, the BBC Philharmonic

▼ Central Manchester Development Corporation area.

- - - City Centre Local Plan Boundary
◼ Financial Core
◻ CMDC Area

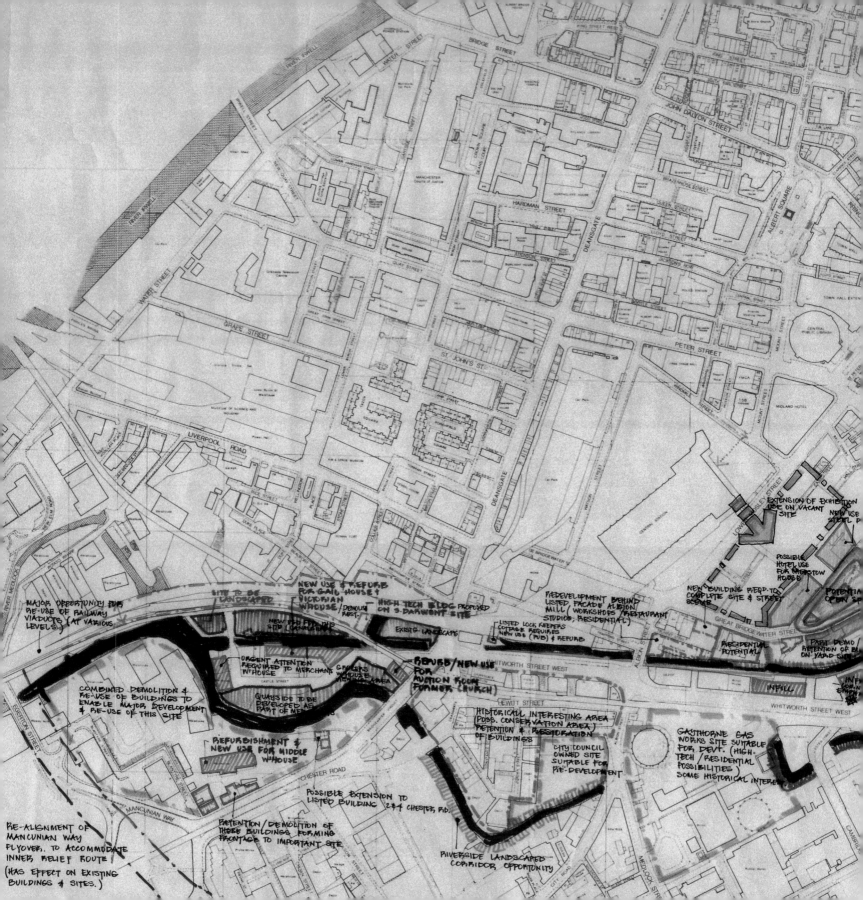

MAJOR OPPORTUNITY FOR
RE-USE OF RAILWAY
VIADUCTS (AT VARIOUS
LEVELS)

SITE TO BE LANDSCAPED

NEW USE & REFURB
FOR GAOL HOUSE &
VICTORIAN
W'HOUSE / DEMOLITION
POSS.

HIGH TECH BLDG PROPOSED
ON S.DARWENT SITE

REDEVELOPMENT BEHIND
LISTED FACADE ALBION
MILL (WORKSHOPS/RESTAURANT
STUDIOS/RESIDENTIAL)

EXTENSION OF EXHIBITION
USE ON VACANT SITE

NEW USE
STEEL P

POSSIBLE
HOTEL USE
FOR CHEPSTOW
HOUSE

NEW BUILDING REQD TO
COMPLETE SITE & STREET
SCENE

POTENTIAL
OPEN SP

NEW USE & THIS
SITE LANDSCAPED

EXISTG. LANDSCAPE

LISTED LOCK KEEPERS
COTTAGE REQUIRES
NEW USE (PUB) & REFURB

GREAT BRIDGEWATER STREET

URGENT ATTENTION
REQUIRED TO MERCHANTS
W'HOUSE

GEORGE'S
W'HOUSE
NEW USE AREA

REFURB/NEW USE
FOR
AUCTION ROOM
(FORMER CHURCH)

RESIDENTIAL
POTENTIAL

PART DEMO
RETENTION OF B
ON YARD SITE

INFILL
INFI

COMBINED DEMOLITION &
RE-USE OF BUILDINGS TO
ENABLE MAJOR DEVELOPMENT
& RE-USE OF THIS SITE

QUAYSIDE TO BE
DEVELOPED AS
PART OF MEAS

HISTORICAL INTERESTING AREA
(POSS. CONSERVATION AREA)
RETENTION & RESTORATION
OF BUILDINGS

WHITWORTH STREET WEST

HEWITT STREET

WHITWORTH STREET WEST

GAYTHORNE GAS
WORKS SITE SUITABLE
FOR DEVT. (HIGH.
TECH/RESIDENTIAL
POSSIBILITIES)
SOME HISTORICAL INTERES

REFURBISHMENT &
NEW USE FOR MIDDLE
W'HOUSE

CHESTER ROAD

CITY COUNCIL
OWNED SITE
SUITABLE FOR
RE-DEVELOPMENT

RE-ALIGNMENT OF
MANCUNIAN WAY
FLYOVER. TO ACCOMMODATE
INNER RELIEF ROUTE
(HAS EFFECT ON EXISTING
BUILDINGS & SITES.)

MANCUNIAN WAY

RETENTION/DEMOLITION OF
THESE BUILDINGS FORMING
FRONTAGE TO IMPORTANT SITE

POSSIBLE EXTENSION TO
LISTED BUILDING 2 & 4 CHESTER RD.

RIVERSIDE LANDSCAPED
CORRIDOR, OPPORTUNITY

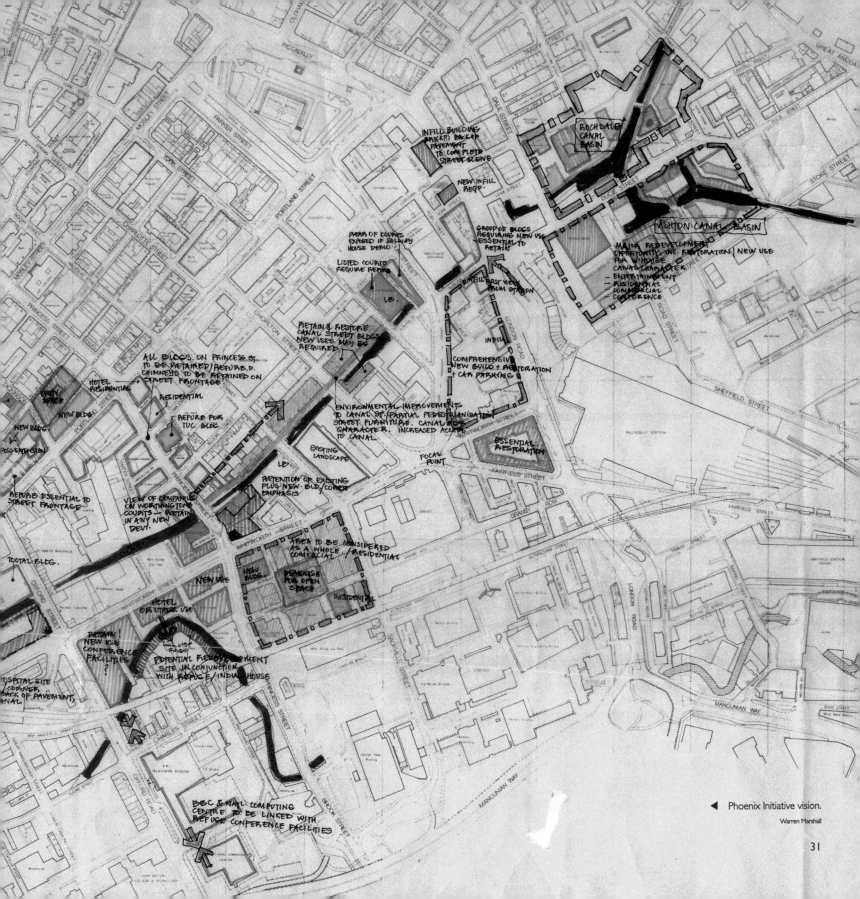

INFILL BUILDING (BRICK) BACK OF PAVEMENT TO COMPLETE STREET SCENE

NEW INFILL REQD

ROCHDALE CANAL BASIN

ASHTON CANAL BASIN

GROUP OF BLDGS REQUIRING NEW USE - ESSENTIAL TO RETAIN

MAJOR REDEVELOPMENT OPPORTUNITY INC. RESTORATION / NEW USE FOR W'HOUSE
· CANAL CHARACTER
· ENTERTAINMENT
· RESIDENTIAL
· COMMERCIAL
· CONFERENCE

REAR OF COURTS EXPOSED IF SOLWAY HOUSE DEMO.

LISTED COURTS REQUIRE REPAIR

INFILL FIRST VIEW FROM STATION

INFILL

COMPREHENSIVE NEW BUILD + RESTORATION + CAR PARKING

RETAIN & RESTORE CANAL STREET BLDGS NEW USES MAY BE REQUIRED

ALL BLDGS. ON PRINCESS ST. TO BE RETAINED / REFURB.D CHIMNEYS TO BE RETAINED ON STREET FRONTAGE

HOTEL / RESIDENTIAL

RESIDENTIAL

OPEN SPACE

NEW BLDG

NEW BLDG / POSS EXTENSION

REFURB FOR TUC BLDG

ENVIRONMENTAL IMPROVEMENTS TO CANAL ST. PARTIAL PEDESTRIANISATION STREET FURNITURE. CANAL-SIDE CHARACTER. INCREASED ACCESS TO CANAL

EXISTING LANDSCAPE

FOCAL POINT

ESSENTIAL RESTORATION

REFURB ESSENTIAL TO STREET FRONTAGE

VIEW OF CAMPANILE ON WORTHINGTON COURTS - RETAIN IN ANY NEW DEVT.

RETENTION OF EXISTING PLUS NEW BLDG / CORNER EMPHASIS

TOOTAL BLDG.

AREA TO BE CONSIDERED AS A WHOLE COMMERCIAL / RESIDENTIAL

NEW USE

NEW BLDG

NEW BLDG

DEMOLISH FOR OPEN SPACE

RESIDENTIAL

HOTEL OR OTHER USE

RETAIN! NEW USE CONFERENCE FACILITIES ?

LINK OVER RACH

POTENTIAL REDEVELOPMENT SITE IN CONJUNCTION WITH REFUGE / INDIA HOUSE

HOSPITAL SITE CORNER, BACK OF PAVEMENT, CANAL

BBC & NAT'L COMPUTING CENTRE TO BE LINKED WITH REFUGE CONFERENCE FACILITIES

◀ Phoenix Initiative vision.

Warren Marshall

31

REBUILDING **MANCHESTER**

▶ City centre financial and professional area, 1990.

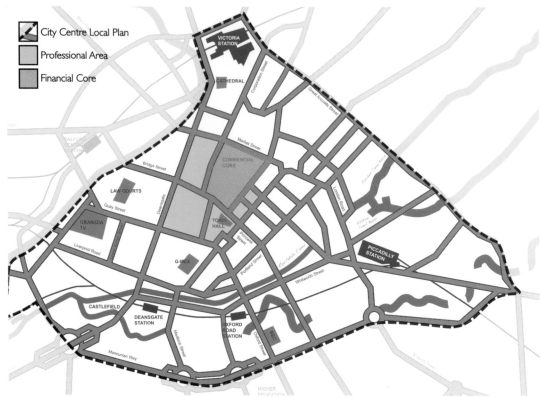

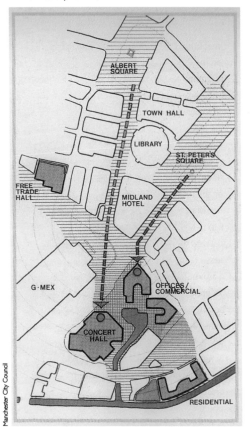

▼ Connection between Bridgewater Hall and the rest of the city centre, 1991.

Manchester City Council

and Manchester Camerata. In addition, it would raise the city's profile by developing a sizeable piece of land in use as temporary car park and expand the commercial core (office buildings 100 and 101 Barbirolli Square formed part of the complex – a crucial part of the scheme both for the city centre and also to secure funding for the whole project). The Hall now hosts over 250 performances a year, including classical music, jazz and world music. The Hall held its first concert on 11 September 1996 and was officially opened by Her Majesty The Queen, accompanied by His Royal Highness the Duke of Edinburgh, on Wednesday 4 December the same year.

It was during this period of creativity that Manchester's decision makers raised the game to a new level. The city chose to bid for the Olympic Games – twice! It was the vision of entrepreneur Sir Bob Scott, who already knew Manchester extremely well, having co-founded a series of cultural projects including the Cornerhouse Cinema and Exhibition Centre, the Royal Exchange Theatre Company and the refurbishment and re-use of the Palace Theatre and Opera House.

He became aware that the Prime Minister, Margaret Thatcher, was willing to entertain the prospect of a UK Olympic bid. This was something that Manchester, without question, could do. He immediately contacted new City Council Leader, Graham Stringer, to discuss a way forward. In 1984 a bid for the 1996 Olympics was launched. While Manchester did not succeed in its bid for the Games (it was placed fifth when the results were announced in Tokyo in 1990), it retained the position of British bid city for the 2000 Games.

▼   100 and 101 Barbirolli Square.

▲ Bridgewater Hall.

▼ Olympic phonecard.

Graham Stringer was very clear about what the city was seeking to achieve when he spoke to the *Manchester Evening News* on 17 February 1993:

'Cities, like sprinters, can't stand still. They have to make progress or go into decline. The great days of heavy industry won't return. We have to find new ways forward. And that's where the Olympic Games come in. Our bid for the 2000 Games is no Town Hall fantasy. It's a calculated move capable of transforming Manchester.'

MANCHESTER 1996
THE BRITISH OLYMPIC BID

DRIVING THE DREAM

▲ 1996 Olympic bid, Albert Square, Town Hall, 1989.

◄▼ 1996 Olympic bid posters.

DRIVING THE DREAM

The ethos of partnership was at the heart of the vision and the relationship with the Government was strong. Prime Minister at the time John Major was quoted in *The Guardian* on 18 February 1993, giving his support and commitment to the bid:

'The Manchester bid is the British bid. It is a national undertaking strongly supported by the British Government. If Manchester is chosen the Government will ensure that all the necessary facilities will be built, partly by private finance and partly by substantial public funding.'

Following the International Olympic Committee election in Monte Carlo on 23 September 1993, Manchester again was not selected to host the Games. But it finished third – a very credible position. An editorial in *The Guardian* published the day after recognised what had been achieved:

'...it's not all about winning. Manchester lost the bid, but regained economic self-confidence in the process...Manchester's motives were economic – the regeneration of a post-industrial city-economy. Success would have been sweet, but failure can be a catalyst for continued change.'

While Manchester did not go on to host the Olympics, there is no doubt it changed people's perceptions of the city. Suddenly, it stopped competing on a regional level with neighbouring towns such as Bolton, Blackburn and Stockport. It was now starting to 'muscle in' with Barcelona, Madrid and Atlanta. As in the 19th century, people were beginning to take Manchester seriously again.

Away from the Olympics, Manchester's urban regeneration strategy continued with the 'City Challenge' programme in 1993, and the launch of the 'City Pride' initiative, which sought to consolidate grant regimes operated by various government departments. Manchester, London and Birmingham were invited to take part in the City Pride initiative with the aim of developing a vision and long-term plan for the regeneration of each city and the surrounding area. In Manchester the private sector, the voluntary sector, the wider community and other public sector agencies all came together to establish a strategic framework for economic and social change and define a series of projects to affect change in the quickest possible time.

The City Pride 'A Focus for the Future' document, published by the city council in 1994, provided a framework for regeneration and development in the city up to 2005:

'Our strategy will build on Manchester's distinctive characteristics and strengths – our industries, our artistic, cultural and sporting institutions, our centres of learning and, above all, our people – to create an area that can compete in its own right, and on its own terms, with other regional capitals in Britain and abroad.'

Another limb that has formed a key part of Manchester's regeneration is Manchester Airport. Originally known as Ringway Airport, it opened on 25 June 1938. After World War Two the use of the airport grew dramatically, and

▼ City Pride.

Manchester City Council

following years of expansion in 1972 it was re-titled 'Manchester International Airport'. It had by this time become a vital part of the city, a conduit for tourism and business – Manchester was a global gateway.

As Manchester moved into the mid-1990s, the city council continued to plan for the future. On 21 July 1995 it published the 'Unitary Development Plan', a document that would frame the council's vision for the next 15 years. The lessons and experiences learnt from the 50 years that had followed the publication of the 1945 City of Manchester Plan were very much embedded within the new document. The preface captured what had been achieved in the city and the targets for the new millennium:

'The city centre, besides being a place where people again wish to reside, is becoming increasingly popular as a regional centre for business and shopping and also for tourism and a wide variety of leisure activities. The recent Olympic bids and the nomination to host the Commonwealth Games in 2002 have helped the city once again to be a player on the world stage. The aim is to make Manchester a truly European regional capital, an international city of outstanding commercial, cultural and creative potential and an area distinguished by the quality of life and sense of well being enjoyed by its residents.'

What had become clear by the time Manchester was awarded the 2002 Commonwealth Games in November 1995 was that the city was on the 'up'. It was successfully re-branding itself, attracting investment and creating strong, tangible partnerships with the public and private sectors. This movement had not gone unnoticed. On 7 May 1996, *The Times* drew attention to the city's renaissance:

'With the decline of industrial Lancashire in the early 20th century Manchester went into eclipse. But over the last two decades the city has experienced a remarkable renaissance that deserves wider recognition…Quietly, Manchester is re-emerging as a great urban centre.'

The events of Saturday 15 June 1996, however, would change part of the city centre forever and, in turn, test the true strength of Manchester City Council's relationship with its public and private sector partners. But first, it is important to present the regeneration of Hulme. While not in the city centre it is an important example of, what was at the time, Manchester's emerging partnership model.

© Aidan O'Rourke - www.aidan.co.uk

▲   Manchester Airport Terminal 1.

▼   The front cover of the Unitary Development Plan, 1995.

THE MANCHESTER PLAN

Manchester City Council

Hulme and the Partnership Model

Hulme, a former industrial suburb immediately south of the city centre (and incidentally the birthplace of the Rolls-Royce) was by the 1980s suffering from severe levels of poverty and deficient environmental conditions. Action was needed, urgently. Funding was provided by the Government under the 'City Challenge' programme on one condition: that Manchester City Council set up an independent company with a blend of public and private experience, which would deliver the project.

The public-private partnership ethos, tested successfully by the CMDC, continued with the establishment of Hulme Regeneration Limited in 1992. Manchester City Council, in partnership with Amec and others, developed and managed the renewal programme. It was largely implemented by two urban-design and architectural advisors, Berridge Lowenbury & Greenberg and Mills Beaumont Leavey Channon (MBLC).

Between 1992 and 1997 some £250 million was invested to redevelop a notorious area of concrete, deck-access council flats, known as the Hulme Crescents, into vibrant, mixed-use, mixed tenure neighbourhoods. It included the refurbishment of 1,650 dwellings, the construction of 2,000 new dwellings, and the creation of development land for commercial activity, including a district shopping centre. Hulme has since become a benchmark for successful urban regeneration that is now internationally recognised and acknowledged.

In an interview published by *Estates Gazette* on 28 May 1994, Ken Knott, now CEO of Ask Developments but at the time of Amec Developments, was adamant about the need for partnership in delivery successful regeneration:

'It would be a fatal mistake to do it any other way. You either do a patchwork job, or you tackle the root causes and put in the foundations to deal with the problem long term.'

The commitment to design quality and place-making ran through many elements of the revitalised Hulme, symbolised by The Hulme Arch bridge designed by Chris Wilkinson — a structure that would link Hulme to the rest of Manchester, both physically and metaphorically.

In an interview published by *Estates Gazette* on 14 March 1998, Howard Bernstein, then Deputy Chief Executive of Manchester City Council, held the Hulme project up as an example of successful place making:

'Hulme gave us the opportunity to take a holistic approach to regeneration. Over the past 10 years we've seen housing-led strategies, employment-led strategies and transport-led strategies. We've tried to produce regeneration-based strategies that incorporate all of those.'

▲ Nash Cresent - taken from Rolls Cresent, 1973.

▼ Demolition of Hulme Flats, 1998.

▼ Hulme Arch.

'120 injured as massive bomb blitzes crowded city centre.'

– Manchester Evening News, 15 June 1996

SATURDAY 15 JUNE 1996

BACKGROUND

15 June 1996 was a warm Saturday morning. England were due to play Scotland at Wembley Stadium in the Euro '96 football tournament later that day. The following evening, Father's Day, Germany were also due to play Russia at Old Trafford as part of the same tournament. All of this meant that Manchester city centre was busy, full of both locals and visitors. It was also the Queen's official birthday, and so the 'Trooping of the Colour' was scheduled to take place in London at 11am. The weekend's events, however, would be overshadowed by a significant security operation.

Four months earlier, on 9 February 1996, the Provisional Irish Republican Army, known more commonly as the IRA, had detonated a half-tonne bomb hidden in a small lorry approximately 80 yards from South Quay Station on the Docklands Light Railway in Canary Wharf, London. Two men, working in a newsagents shop directly opposite the explosion, were killed while 39 people required hospital treatment due to blast injuries and falling glass. Critically, it signalled the end of the 'cessation of military operations' ordered by the IRA leadership in 1994.

Further attacks took place across London during March and April 1996, but thankfully without injury. The threat of a further, major event from the IRA on the mainland was at the time considered to be very high, and hence police were mounting a substantial security operation in London. What was not known, however, was where or when the next attack would take place.

Back in Manchester city centre, Greater Manchester Police were on patrol and performing routine checks of the city centre. At **07.00am** officers walked along Corporation Street and past the Marks & Spencer store opposite the Arndale Centre. The street at the time was clear, with no activity. Just over two hours later, at 09.20am, people had started to arrive in the heart of the city centre. At this time, a Ford Cargo van, registration number C214 ACL with a distinctive plywood door at the rear, was spotted on video turning from St Mary's Gate into Corporation Street. Two minutes later, at **09.22am**, the van stopped outside Marks & Spencer.

▲ The bomb truck parked on Corporation Street, Saturday 15 June 1996.

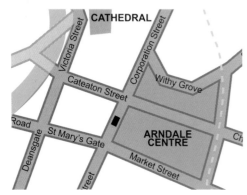

▲ The location of the bomb truck.

▶ The bomb truck on Corporation Street, taken from a police helicopter.

Two men wearing sunglasses and anoraks were spotted leaving the van. They then walked northwards towards Cateaton Street and the cathedral, heading in the direction of Victoria Station. They went on to join a third man who was sitting in a burgundy-coloured Ford Granada on Cathedral Street. The vehicle set off and turned right onto Fennel Street and continued north, making its way out of the city centre.

A traffic warden, only minutes after the van had parked up outside Marks & Spencer, noticed the vehicle, which was parked on a double-yellow line. A ticket was placed on the windscreen. There was no sign of the driver or any passengers. Fifteen minutes later, at **09.41am**, a man with an Irish accent contacted Granada TV and Greater Manchester Police and warned of a bomb located in one of three areas: the Arndale Centre, the Corn Exchange and Marks & Spencer. It was due to go off in an hour. Similar calls were received at Manchester General Hospital, Sky TV, Salford University, the offices of RTE Television in Ireland and the Garda. Crucially, the caller gave a codeword used by the IRA, and Greater Manchester Police quickly concluded that the calls were genuine. The Crime Management Unit, part of Greater Manchester Police, immediately entered 'Code Red', and emergency procedures were put into action. Manchester was well placed to react quickly to a terrorist attack as the city council had a dedicated emergency control centre. The city, after all, had witnessed an attack from the IRA on 3 December 1992 when two bombs exploded – one at Parsonage Gardens and one near the cathedral – injuring 65 people. Thankfully no one was killed.

Two key security procedures were implemented: Firstly, inner and outer cordons were established and the police, in collaboration with major store security personnel, began to evacuate the 80,000 people estimated to be in the city centre at the time. The inner cordon was set at 400–500m from the suspect vehicle on Corporation Street, while the outer cordon encircled the city centre, following the line of the inner relief route. Secondly, the army bomb-disposal team was summoned from their base in Liverpool.

Back in the city centre, by **10.00am** shops and offices began to clear, although there was resistance being shown by some members of the public. PC Gary Hartley of Greater Manchester Police was one of the first policemen on the scene. Upon being interviewed by BBC North West as part of a programme called *Close Up North*, broadcast in October 1996, he outlined the difficulties the police had faced:

'We were trying to get the area sterile. People weren't listening to us. We were putting tape across the road, people were going underneath the tape to take short cuts to where they wanted to go, which was quite frustrating when we knew the danger they were putting themselves into. We didn't know when the bomb was due to go off; we didn't know what size it was, how big it was, we had no idea. We just had time on our side to get people moving.'

A further constraint to the evacuation procedure was the absence of a comprehensive CCTV system in the city centre. At the time, such a scheme was being planned but was not in place. Much of the evacuation was undertaken at street level by officers using loudhailers, while other members of the police monitored events using traffic cameras. Above the streets a police helicopter also monitored the evacuation of shoppers and the target vehicle on Corporation Street.

By **11.00am** many of the people in the city centre had been evacuated. The police also announced that the Arndale Centre was clear. At this time the bomb-disposal team arrived from Liverpool and assembled near Sam's Chop House at Back Pool Fold off Cross Street, some 200 yards from the target vehicle. The Explosive Ordnance Disposal (EOD), a team specially trained to deal with the disarmament and disposal of high-explosive munitions, went into operation.

A robotic device was sent forward by the EOD from Cross Street onto Corporation Street at **11.10am** to investigate and defuse the bomb. The device was armed with a gun, which would fire rounds of ammunition and explosive charges, in turn defusing the device. There would be two explosions: the first smaller than the second. Once the device had reached the truck and started to try and defuse the bomb, police officers were shocked to see a woman appear on the footbridge above the target vehicle, having emerged from the Arndale Centre. Thankfully, as the first controlled explosion took place she ran back into the Centre.

As the robotic device continued to try and eliminate the risk of the bomb exploding, it became clear to officers that time was running out. Speaking to the *Manchester Evening News* in an article published on 16 June 1996, photographer Paul Sanders, who at the time was standing just 50 yards from the site, recounted his story:

REBUILDING **MANCHESTER**

▶ Corporation Street, the detonator approaches the bomb truck.

▶ The bomb truck on Corporation Street, taken from a police helicopter. The pedestrian footbridge connecting Marks & Spencer and Arndale Centre is visible above the truck. The office building, Longridge House, can be seen to the right.

▶ 11.17am – the truck explodes.

▼ The bomb-damaged area.

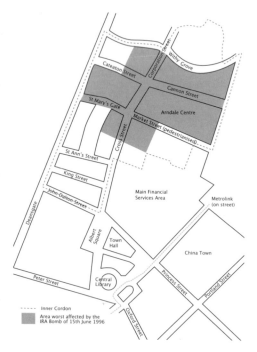

'A police officer was constantly on his radio, and three bomb disposal people were going backwards and forwards with equipment. Suddenly one of them ran off to a wall where some building workers were leaning over and shouted "get back, get back".'

At 11.17am the bomb exploded.

THE DEVASTATION

The shockwave from the bomb, which was estimated to have weighed 3,300lbs, devastated buildings nearby and up to one mile from the explosion.

Due to the fantastic work undertaken by the police, 80,000 people had successfully been evacuated from the heart of the city centre. Eighty-one ambulances from Manchester, Merseyside and West Yorkshire raced to the scene, and just over 200 people were taken to hospital. Fourteen people were seriously injured but, thankfully, no one was killed.
At the seat of the bomb on Corporation Street a crater was left, 15ft wide. Buildings immediately adjacent to the bomb were decimated. Longridge House, home of the Royal Insurance Group, took the full force of the explosion. Next door the Marks & Spencer store, along with the six-storey office block Michael House, immediately became a condemned site.

MEN Syndication

▲ Aerial photograph taken on 15 June 1996 showing the devastation following the bomb.

REBUILDING **MANCHESTER**

▲ Marks & Spencer store, corner of Cross Street and Corporation Street.

▶ Longridge House and the crater left by the truck bomb.

▶ Corporation Street and the devastated Arndale Centre.

▼ View from Deansgate to Shambles Square.

Cameraman Martin Smith was part of the team working in Thompson House (formerly known as Maxwell House) opposite the Corn Exchange:

'I was part of the ITV *Prime Suspect* film crew, and we had several sets in Maxwell House. We were due to go and use the sets the week of the bomb; we were rescheduled due to the mess. Design had to rebuild everything, since the blast literally moved everything to one side of the building. Once we got in the sets were OK, but the building had lots of blast signs; rippled tiled floors, and partition walls had been blown out.'

The Arndale Centre's frontage running along Corporation Street was devastated, with tiles torn away by the blast. The pedestrian footbridge which connected the Centre with Marks & Spencer was blown to pieces. It immediately became the symbol of the attack, appearing on news bulletins and the front page of newspapers. Inside the Arndale Centre many shops were badly damaged. Ray Bunting of architects Ratcliff Partnership was one of the first to go into the building shortly after the attack:

'It was like a scene from a Stanley Kubrick film. There was smashed glass everywhere and dummies from various shop units strewn on the floor. Alarms were blaring and music videos were still playing on monitors in some of the shops. It was eerie to say the least.'

The physical effects of the blast were not limited to post-war buildings. Like a tornado, it blew its way through many parts of Manchester's built heritage. Across the road from Longridge House, the blast had rolled up the street and into the Corn Exchange. 'It got one hell of a pasting' said Manchester City Council architect Bob King in an interview with *The Guardian* published on 4 July 1996. 'The dome was lifted off by the blast.'

▲ Longridge House (left) and Marks & Spencer (right).

The Ratcliff Partnership Ltd

REBUILDING **MANCHESTER**

▲ Nicholas Witchell tells the nation about the bombing on *BBC News*.

▲ Cathedral Street looking towards Longridge House. Corn Exchange on the left, Manchester Cathedral on the right.

▶ Bomb damage to Benetton, inside the Arndale Centre.

Similarly, the Royal Exchange building in St Ann's Square, which comprised shops, offices and the Royal Exchange Theatre, was badly affected. In an article published by *BBC News* on 19 November 1998, Joanna Lord, who was working in the theatre box office at the time, spoke about the impact;

'The worst thing about it was that you didn't hear the bomb – you felt it first. It was a huge "pop" then you felt the force…and the last thing was this bang. I didn't see the damage until it was on the news. I just cried, it was awful.'

Initial surveys suggested that while there was significant superficial damage to the Royal Exchange, the building appeared to have escaped relatively unscathed; however, further investigations soon revealed that the roof of the building had 'jumped' in the blast and landed 2in askew. There was a real concern that the building may have been weakened structurally, which could have led to its demolition.

While the Marks & Spencer building had taken the main impact of the bomb, the ensuing blast funnelled between buildings and hit the main gable end of The Old Wellington pub – a Scheduled Ancient Monument located in Shambles Square. All the windows were shattered, and the blast pressure lifted the roof slightly, pushing out the upper timber walls. A survey following the bomb revealed that the heavy roof stone slabs in the building had cracked and slipped. The adjoining Sinclair's Oyster Bar also suffered extensive structural damage.

The Ratcliff Partnership Ltd

◄ Bomb damage to Thomas Cook, Arndale Centre/ Market Street.

The Ratcliff Partnership Ltd

◄ Bomb damage to Freeman Hardy Willis, Arndale Centre.

The Ratcliff Partnership Ltd

▲◀ Bomb damage inside the Arndale Centre.

▼ Bomb damage inside the Corn Exchange.

Superficial damage was much more widespread. St Ann's Church in St Ann's Square sustained major damage to the gallery, windows, main door and the vestry. Windows were blown out of shops on Deansgate along with the Corn Exchange, Chetham's School of Music, Victoria Station and Manchester Cathedral to the north. The remainder of the Shambles Square Market Place, which comprised offices and retail space, known as Shambles East and Shambles West, was also badly damaged, as was the Arndale Tower.

The damage in overall terms was considerable. 742,000sq ft (69,000m²) of retail floorspace was damaged, along with 613,000sq ft (57,000m²) of office space. Other parts of the city's infrastructure were also significantly affected; the city centre's largest bus station based in the Arndale Centre was also closed for business. It would never re-open.

▲ Bomb damage inside the Corn Exchange. Note the clock above the door which stopped at 11.17am – the time the bomb went off.

◄ Tiles removed from the wall by bomb damage inside the Corn Exchange.

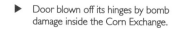

▶ Door blown off its hinges by bomb damage inside the Corn Exchange.

▲ Bomb damage, Royal Exchange Theatre.

REBUILDING **MANCHESTER**

Stephen Welsh

▶ The view along Corporation Street towards the bomb site. Longridge House on the right and Arndale Centre on the left.

Why was it called 'Shambles Square'?

According to the Chambers Dictionary, the word 'shamble' means 'a butcher's market stall, a flesh-market, hence, a slaughterhouse'.

Evidence suggests that the word came from the old butchers' market in York; a street of butchers where meat was prepared. The sights and smells would have been remarkable as blood, pieces of meat and offal ran into the gutter.

Hence, it was the location of Manchester's original meat market and a place of historic value.

The Ratcliff Partnership Ltd

▶ Shambles Square and damaged office block.

◀ Inside Macintosh House, Shambles Square.

◀ Windows blown out of Arndale Tower by the bomb blast (taken from inside the Arndale Centre).

Standing Tall

Although the blast caused significant harm to buildings in the immediate vicinity, there were two pieces of Manchester's streetscape that refused to bow to the attack.

The first was a red post box located outside Marks & Spencer on Corporation Street. Amazingly, it withstood the force of the bomb and was restored and put back in its original location in 1999. The mail in the box was also unharmed.

The second was a set of traffic lights on the junction of Cross Street and Market Street. Even though all the glass was blown out and there was a shrapnel hole though the base, the 10ft traffic light carried on offering instructions. It was subsequently cleaned up and proudly put on display at the Museum of Science and Industry.

© Aidan O'Rourke - www.aidan.co.uk

▲ Postbox unharmed by the bomb.

▼ Damaged traffic light at the junction of Cross Street and Market Street.

▼ The traffic light on display at the Museum of Science and Industry.

The Ratcliff Partnership Ltd

Norma Fernandez

© George Fairbairn

◀ The entrance to the former Arndale Bus Station on Shudehill, before the bomb.

THE RESPONSE

As the city centre awoke to the sound of alarms and sirens on Sunday 16 June 1996, the principles, processes and partnerships established by Manchester City Council in the years before the attack were immediately harnessed and put into action. To achieve stability there were two priorities:

PRIORITY ONE: BUSINESSES AND RESIDENTS

The first was to assist and, in some cases relocate, the 670 businesses that had been directly affected by the attack. The first 24 hours after the bomb were frantic. Between 5,000 and 10,000 people descended on the Town Hall, wanting to know where they would trade and how they could retrieve their personal possessions (such as house and car keys) from the bomb-damaged area. The disruption also affected residents in the Cromford Court apartments located above the Arndale Centre, managed by Northern Counties Housing Association. It was not a short-term solution – they would have to be relocated and re-housed.

Many small, independent traders were crippled by the bomb, particularly those in the Corn Exchange. Cathy Malcolm was the owner of a shop called 'Pygar' which sold, among other things, lava lamps and clothes.

REBUILDING **MANCHESTER**

▲ The Corn Exchange.

During an interview that featured on BBC North West's *Close Up North* programme in October 1996 she explained how the bomb had crippled many small businesses:

'I'm a small trader who had a shop in the centre of Manchester in the Corn Exchange. It was a very interesting shop. I'd built it up for years, my whole livelihood was in that shop, and one day the IRA came and blew it up.'

Cathy, sadly, was not alone. Many traders in the Corn Exchange were unfortunate enough to have no terrorism insurance.

The loss of premises was not limited to small businesses. Marks & Spencer immediately had to find new retail space, as did other household names such as Top Shop, Argos and HMV and two businesses that had been unlucky enough to open new shops in Manchester literally weeks before the attack: clothes retailer USC on Market Street and Häagen-Dazs at Shambles Square. The same rule applied to many of the businesses that occupied office space; mainly those in the Arndale Tower, the Corn Exchange, Longridge House and Shambles Square.

PRIORITY TWO: REBUILDING THE CITY CENTRE

Manchester City Council immediately called upon the strong working relationship it had established with the Government. Home Secretary Michael Howard visited the city on Monday 17 June 1996 to witness the devastation, but it was Michael Heseltine, Deputy Prime Minister at the time, who without question was best placed to assist and provide expertise. In the

▶ Bomb-damaged Häagen-Dazs unit, Shambles Square.

Danny O'Neill, Mr Magoo and a Goldfish

There were stories in the weeks that followed that provided a sense of proportion to the disaster. Danny O'Neill, a 77-year old RAF veteran, remained in his Cromford Court flat above the Arndale Centre for three days after the blast, because he had 'flu. When the caretaker knocked on his door, warning him of the blast, Danny thanked him – and went back to bed. Three days later Northern Housing Association staff was stunned to receive a call from Danny saying he was feeling better and would like advice in terms of what he should do. In an interview with the *Manchester Evening News* published on 11 July 1997 he captured the event wonderfully by saying:

▲   Danny O'Neill.

'You can overdo this danger business. I never really understood what all the fuss was about.'

On 16 July 1996, *The Independent* shared other stories of note. There were calls about a 20-year-old parrot called Mr Magoo which, one week on, was still in Paddy's Rat and Carrot Irish theme pub located in the Arndale Centre along Corporation Street – literally, opposite the bomb site. A member of staff at the Orange phone shop on Market Street was also surprised to receive a call from the building control officer two weeks after the explosion to say that the fish were still alive in their ornamental tank. 'If you tell us where the fish food is, we'll feed them' said the voice at the other end of the line.

wake of the 1981 Toxteth riots in Liverpool, he had taken three weeks off as Environment Secretary and moved to Liverpool in an attempt to get under the skin of the problem. Peter Kilfoyle, a Labour Party organiser in the 1980s, spoke highly of Heseltine's achievements in Liverpool, citing him in a *Guardian* interview on 16 May 2004 as someone who 'cut through the crap and got things done'. Heseltine's drive went on to bring about the successful redevelopment of the Albert Dock and, through the novelty of a Garden Festival, regenerated acres of derelict land.

He made his first visit to Manchester city centre on Wednesday 26 June 1996 and toured the shattered centre. Having already described the attack in a *Manchester Evening News* interview on the same day as an 'appalling and disgraceful perpetration', it was clear that he too saw the damaged core as a wonderful opportunity to rectify the hasty mistakes of post-war development. Most importantly, however, he recognised the national importance of the city of Manchester. In an article published by *The Guardian* on 27 June 1996 he described the situation as 'an opportunity perhaps unique, to rebuild and recreate the centre of one of England's great cities.'

Speaking to the *Manchester Evening News* on the day of his visit, new City Council Leader Richard Leese was keen for Michael Heseltine to come and listen. He immediately saw the opportunity to recreate the Hulme regeneration model:

'I would like by the end of today to feel confident that the government was going to set up a task force to deal with what is a national responsibility. The people of Manchester have already suffered through no fault of their own. They should not suffer in the future through having to meet the cost of putting right the damage. The Deputy Prime Minister would be foolish not to come and listen and, to some extent, reserve judgment.'

▶ *Manchester Evening News* front page,
Wednesday 26 June 1996.

Manchester Evening News

Final m.

Wednesday June 26 1996   *Founded 1868*   *A friend dropping in*   30p   SOCCER CITY 96

VIDEO FIT
OUR GUIDE TO THE BEST WORKOUTS
WOMEN: Pages 12 and 13

1966
AND ALL THAT !
TV: Page 31

MANCHESTER'S HEARTFELT PLEA TO HESELTINE:

HOW YOU CAN SAVE OUR CITY

Big aid rescue package is on the way

MICHAEL Heseltine today indicated that a substantial government aid package is on the way for bomb-shattered Manchester.

He toured the devastated shopping centre and called the terrorist attack "an appalling and disgraceful perpetration."

Then he promised: "There is bound to be extra money."

He did not know the form or the scale of the package. However, he promised to return to the city next week after reporting back to Mr Major when "we might be able to take the process further."

Mr Heseltine also announced that the government would be giving £50,000 to the Lord Mayor's Emergency Fund as a "spontaneous reaction" to help cases of immediate hardship.

He stressed: "It must not be seen in any way as the government's response to the enormity of what has happened here.

"I understand that people in the private sector have offered to match the government's contribution and will produce the equivalent cash. It would then be up to local people to deal with cases of hardship."

Speaking of the government's ultimate financial aid Mr Heseltine said: "It will be a figure of a quite different order of magnitude. There are just very big questions.

"There is bound to be extra money that we don't know the form of or the scale. I don't intend to give any indication today."

MANCHESTER today demanded a master-plan from Michael Heseltine for the rebuilding of its bomb-blitzed heart.

City leaders told the Deputy Prime Minister as he toured the wrecked shopping centre they want:

● A task force headed by him or a high-ranking Cabinet colleague to spearhead the £500m renewal drive;

● A clear declaration of support of government commitment as a confidence booster for the business community;

● Rapid decisions on how the master-plan will be delivered, and;

● Immediate help for small traders threatened with ruin.

Howard Bernstein, the city's deputy chief executive, said today: "Manchester wants and needs a speedy and effective response from the highest levels of government.

"It must be dealt with at a national level — not a regional level. This bomb has devastated the very heart of the city.

"This is not just about the future of Manchester — the blast has affected the principal shopping core for the whole of north west England."

City leaders want details from Mr Heseltine about methods and machinery that government will use to tackle the problems faced by businesses. Council leader Richard Leese said: "I would like by the end of today to feel confident that the government was going to set up a task force to deal with what is a national responsibility.

"The people of Manchester have already suffered through no fault of their own. They should not suffer in the future through having to meet the cost of putting right the damage."

Coun Leese, who met Mr Heseltine

■ Touring the terror target: Mr Heseltine and Mr Burt, foreground, inspect the devastation with city leaders today

By Ray King, Janine Watson and Ian Craig

with business leaders this morning and staged private talks later, said: "The Deputy Prime Minister would be foolish not to come and listen and, to some extent, reserve judgment.

"But the government has already had a week and a half of input from the Minister for Manchester and from civil servants."

Deputy leader Martin Pagel said: "It's not just a question of Mr Heseltine listening. The small business peope most at risk will want to listen to his answers to the question what is the government going to do over the next two weeks to

save them." On his way to Manchester with Minister for Manchester Alistair Burt, Mr Heseltine said he had seen no fewer than six copies of the *Evening News* open letter to John Major. It appealed for help with the rebuilding of the shopping centre including the setting up a task force and urged Ministers to come to the city to see the problems.

"The Prime Minister is obviously aware that a lot of effort is being made by many people to cope with the aftermath of the outrage," said Mr Heseltine.

"But he wanted to be sure that where

this might impact on the government, that the government was helping in any way that was right for us.

In Parliament, the government is under pressure to set up a special compensation fund, similar to the Compensation Agency in Northern Ireland, to cover the cost of terrorist damage.

At least 100 businesses in the city centre were not covered by insurance against terrorism.

Mr Heseltine said he was not ruling any ideas in, or ruling them out. He confirmed that the compensation arrangements in Ulster did not apply on the mainland. But he said there were special government-backed insurance schemes available.

■ City fightback: P2 &P3

WEATHER 2 BMDs 26 DIARY 29 POSTBAG 30 TV 31-34 BUSINESS: 8 PAGES

MEN Syndication

Heseltine's impact was prompt. A week later, on Wednesday 3 July 1996, he made his second visit to Manchester and, in turn, announced a £21 million aid package. He also announced that the Government and Manchester City Council had, as requested by Richard Leese, established a task force comprising professionals from both the public and private sector. This would be known as Manchester Millennium Limited. This built upon the model of Manchester's previous urban regeneration experience, demonstrated successfully in Hulme, and would be responsible for developing and managing the recovery strategy.

Like Hulme Regeneration Limited, it would contain a blend of experience. The company would be led by Sir Alan Cockshaw, with Richard Leese as Deputy Chair and Howard Bernstein as Chief Executive. The board also included other members such as Sir David Trippier (Chair of Marketing Manchester), Marianne Neville-Rolfe, (Regional Director, Government Office North West), Kath Robinson (Deputy Leader, Manchester City Council) and Tony Strachan (Agent, Bank of England).

What was crucial was that they all knew – and trusted – each other, having worked together in the past. This partnership approach was vital. Once again, high-quality design was an absolute priority – only the best would do. This would be secured by way of an international urban design competition.

INTERNATIONAL URBAN DESIGN COMPETITION

The competition was formally launched by Manchester Millennium on 17 July 1996. Expressions of interest were to be submitted by 23 August 1996, and a shortlist was announced, with further submissions expected by 18 October 1996. The results, and chosen masterplan team, would be announced at the beginning of November 1996.

The area covered by the competition brief totalled 24 hectares and was bound by St Ann's Square, the River Irwell and Piccadilly Station. There were two areas: the bomb core, devastated by the blast; and the outer area, where further regeneration initiatives would flow in the years after the immediate rebuilding.

The brief called for a coherent and attractive area, with emphasis placed upon the quality of public open space, a gateway to the area, the exploitation of the River Irwell and the area's historic buildings and the integration of the medieval core (anchored by the Cathedral and Chetham's School of Music) and pedestrianised links to the retail core. Crucially the trading of the Arndale Centre was not to be disrupted. A key requirement of the brief was to ensure proposals were deliverable in a phased manner, with the majority being delivered in a three-year timeframe. The aim of the rebuilding and regeneration of the city centre was clear: replace what was lost with something superior; strengthen the city's position as the regional capital; and compete with the emerging Trafford Centre, due to open in September 1998. The shopping centre, located in the Metropolitan Borough of Trafford in Greater Manchester and six miles (10km) west of Manchester city centre, was one of the longest and most expensive planning applications since the introduction of the Town and Country Planning Act in 1947. With proposed floorspace of almost 1.6 million sq ft (150,000m^2) in an out-of-town location, the decision was elevated to the House of Lords and planning permission was eventually granted.

'We want to see a development and investment framework established which creates an architecturally distinctive core, which is of urban character, and is responsive to the access needs of the young and old, people with disabilities, and which is physically and socially integrated with the rest of the City. Our objective is to maximise private investment and stimulate economic activity. The framework must promote the widest possible range of opportunities for people to live, shop, work and relax safely; and where activity can take place at most times of day and night.'

– Manchester Millennium Limited

Manchester City Council

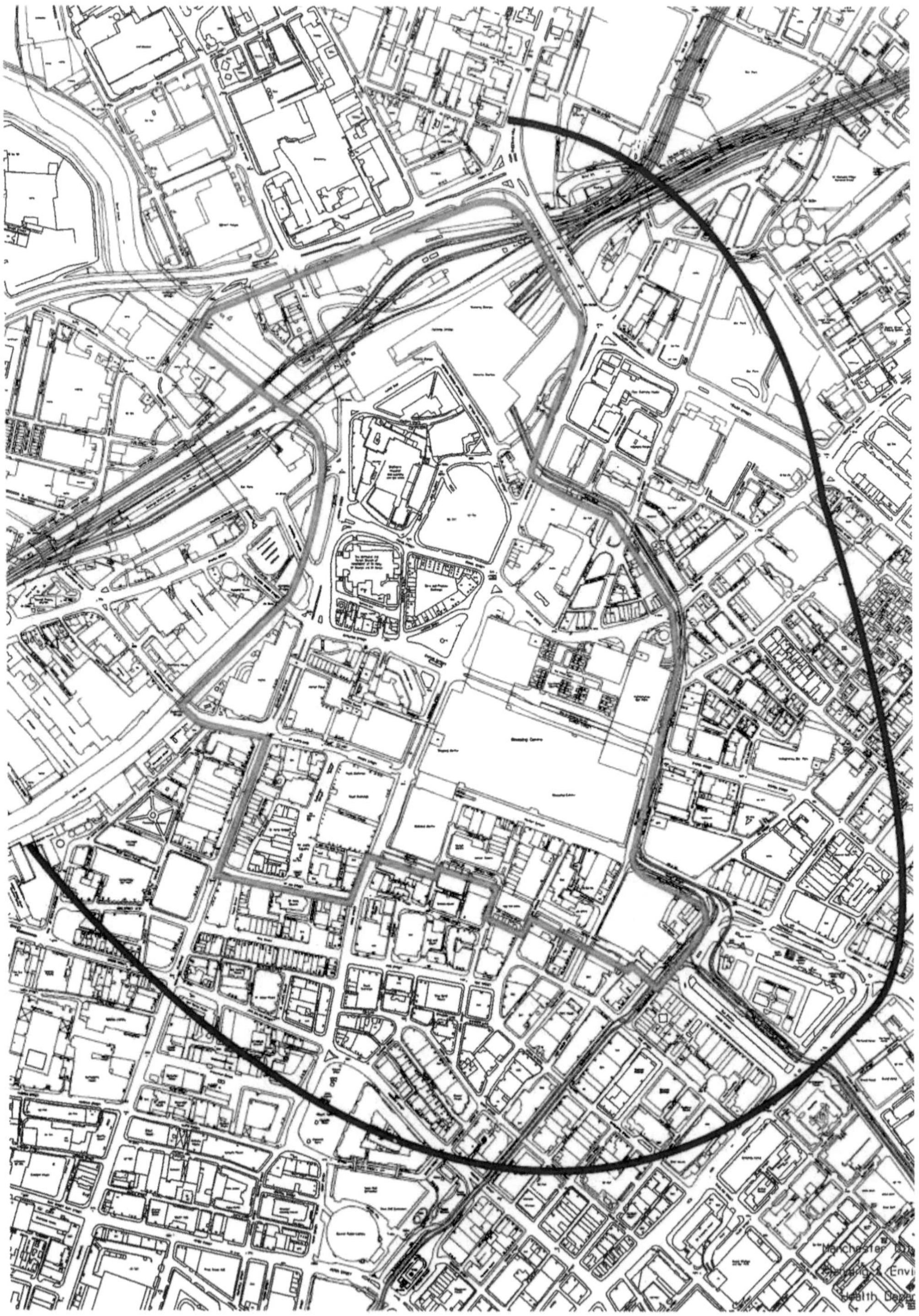

Core Study Area

Surrounding Area

▶ Study area, international urban design competition.

With modern retail units and free car parking, the shopping centre was a perceived threat to Manchester city centre. This put pressure on the city to rebuild and retain its existing retail tenants, businesses, shoppers and residents, and do it quickly (ideally, by the new millennium and certainly in time for the 2002 Commonwealth Games).

The first round of the competition closed with 27 submissions. A shortlist of five was announced by Manchester Millennium on 21 September 1996. Property journal *Estates Gazette* included an article on the competition on 26 October 1996, summarising the shortlisted entries as illustrates over the following pages.

THE SHORTLIST

Halliday Meecham Architects

An extension of the Arndale Centre and a glazed atrium over a pedestrianised Corporation Street were proposed. The Old Wellington and Sinclair's Oyster Bar were discarded in favour of a new internal retail environment. Great attention was also paid to the River Irwell, with a proposed riverboat enclosure facing the Cathedral.

First published in Estates Gazette, 26 October 1996

What is a Masterplan?

A masterplan sets out the framework and vision for a large area (such as a neighbourhood or district), providing a context and a series of parameters for the individual projects that follow. They are not rigid blueprints like the 1945 City of Manchester Plan – quite the opposite. They generally offer room for manoeuvre and creative thinking when designing and delivering the pieces site by site.

Once a masterplan is in place for a defined area, planning applications for the individual sites can be prepared and submitted for approval. Once approved, development can commence shortly after (subject to dotting i's and crossing t's).

◄ Halliday Meecham's shortlisted entry.

First published in Estates Gazette, 26 October 1996

▲ Edaw's shortlisted entry.

Edaw

A new square was proposed, bound by the Arndale Centre, the Corn Exchange and a new Marks & Spencer, linked to St Ann's Square by a pedestrian boulevard (titled New Cathedral Street). An extension of the Arndale Centre to the north was also proposed, along with an element of mixed-use. A cultural building and leisure development was planned for Maxwell House, along with a new transport interchange.

Building Design Partnership (BDP)

The bomb core was broken down into new public spaces, one centred around the Sinclair's Oyster Bar and the Old Wellington, and the other opening up a space directly opposite the new Corporation Street entrance to the Arndale.

The riverfront was addressed through the provision of Cathedral Gardens, while a connection was made between the Cathedral and River Irwell.

First published in Estates Gazette, 26 October 1996

▲ Building Design Partnership's shortlisted entry.

▲   Manchester First's shortlisted entry to the design competition.

First published in *Estates Gazette, 26 October 1996*

Manchester First

Corporation Street would be the home of a new entertainment and arts centre. Retail and arts centres would be included along the River Irwell, with the former Exchange Station railway arches along Deansgate brought back into use. A new complex could be opened to the north of Cannon Street, including retail, a food market and an entertainment centre.

► Llewellyn Davies' shortlisted entry.

First published in Estates Gazette, 26 October 1996

Llewelyn Davies

A new market square would be placed between Chetham's School of Music, Victoria Station and the Corn Exchange while a Cathedral piazza would link to the River Irwell. The bus station would be placed behind Victoria Station. The Arndale would receive a new façade and arcades, plus a winter garden, replacing Market Street and Cannon Street.

The five competing designs went on public display at Manchester Town Hall on Friday 25 October 1996 through to Sunday 27 October 1996. On Tuesday 5 November 1996 Edaw was announced as the winner by Manchester Millennium, with BDP in second place.

THE CHALLENGE

By the time of the bomb Manchester was emerging from the crippling effects of economic decline, but activity in the city centre was still constrained to the retail and financial district. There were emerging distinct localities in the Northern Quarter, the Village (at the time widely known as the Gay Village), China Town and Castlefield, but to a certain extent these areas were still set apart from the city centre. Despite post-war endeavours to introduce landmark commercial developments, such as the CIS Tower and Piccadilly Plaza, and expand the city-centre core, they stood as a bleak dividing line between the city centre and extensive areas of inner-city decay. This trend was not exclusive to Manchester – at the time this was characteristic of many British cities in the 1970s and 1980s.

One of the greatest challenges faced by the masterplan was, therefore, that of 'connectivity' at street level – in other words, the ability for pedestrians to easily navigate the city centre and get from, say, St Ann's Square to the Arndale Centre and then Victoria Station. The bomb-damaged area was notoriously poor for connectivity, with closed spaces and dark alleys – Shambles Square and the northern part of the Arndale Centre being two of the worst offenders. This connectivity problem was illustrated by the arrival into the city centre when travelling by rail. Upon arrival at either Piccadilly or Victoria Station visitors who did not know Manchester would have to walk for at least five minutes to find an area with life and activity.

As a marker of a city centre that had suffered from a stagnant property market, portions of prime land in Manchester were host to a multitude of temporary car parks, often containing pot holes filled with water and uneven surfaces. They were dotted at regular intervals within the inner relief route. And it was not limited to vacant sites. It included buildings that represented Manchester's industrial past, such as the Great Northern Warehouse on Deansgate.

▲ The northern part of the Arndale Centre before redevelopment, 2002.

▲ Shambles Square alleyway, 1997.

▲ Shambles Square, 1997.

MEN Syndication

◄ Manchester city centre before the bomb.

65

This was typical of the area that would be affected by the bomb. It was littered with piecemeal development, vacant buildings, temporary car parks, cleared land, non-descript post-war architecture and had a lack of connectivity on foot and by car with the rest of the centre.

THE SOLUTION

The Edaw team, which consisted of architects Simpson Associates (now 'Ian Simpson Architects'), Benoy (retail development) and Alan Baxter (transportation and engineering), was spearheaded by Jason Prior and understood Manchester city centre and its complexities. While the bomb had unlocked a whole host of opportunities, there were a number of challenges. Six objectives were outlined by the team for the redesign of the city centre:

- Restore and enhance the retail core.
- Stimulate and diversify the city's economic base.
- Develop an integrated transport strategy.
- Create a quality city core fit for the 21st century.
- Create a living city by increasing the residential population.
- Create a distinctive millennium quarter.

At the heart of the masterplan was a critical north-south connection which would drive through the heart of Shambles Square, in turn connecting St Ann's Square with the Cathedral and the proposed 'medieval quarter' to the rear of the Corn Exchange.

DELIVERING THE MASTERPLAN

No matter how glossy or grandiose a vision or masterplan may be, there is a due process that is unavoidable – that of securing planning permission. Without permission very little development and construction can take place. Accordingly, the city council and Manchester Millennium Limited published a document known as Supplementary Planning Guidance (SPG) for the bomb-damaged area. This was based upon Edaw's winning masterplan and provided a framework for those developers and landowners wishing to prepare and submit planning applications.

The guidance translated the masterplan into a series of policies and objectives – in turn providing applicants with a degree of certainty:

'This guidance will be used in the determination of planning and other applications and, therefore, applicants will be expected to demonstrate how their proposals address the issues that it covers. Also, applicants are advised to refer to the full text of the Unitary Development Plan and the City Development Guide, together with relevant guidance from central government, for example, Planning Policy Guidance notes.'

THE MANCHESTER MODEL

The handling of this process is what makes Manchester so different and so successful. The city council committed to determining all planning applications within a period of eight weeks. To provide a useful context local planning

AECOM Design + Planning

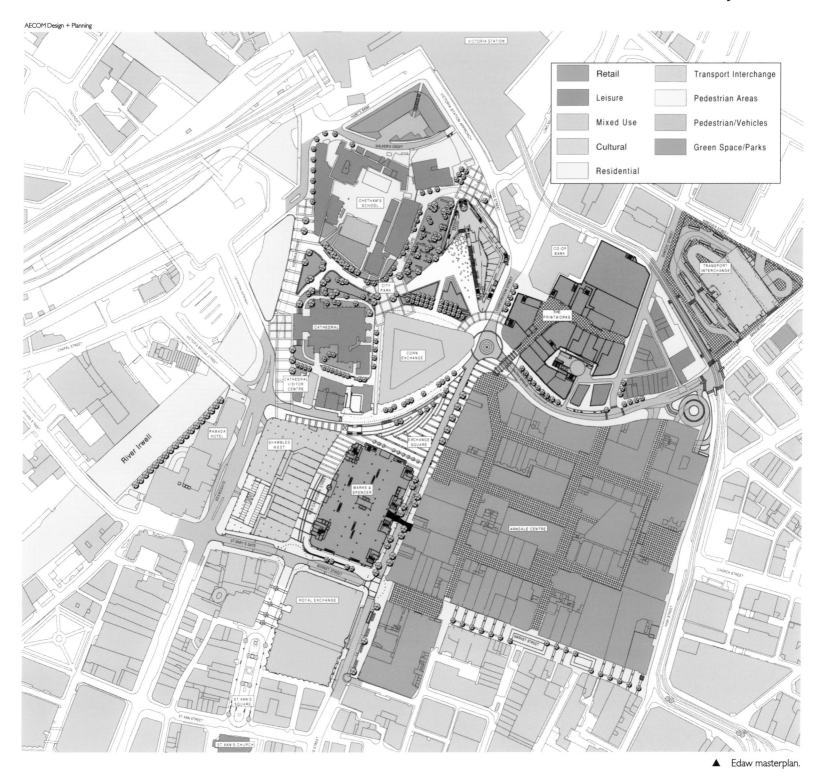

	Retail		Transport Interchange
	Leisure		Pedestrian Areas
	Mixed Use		Pedestrian/Vehicles
	Cultural		Green Space/Parks
	Residential		

▲ Edaw masterplan.

authorities are, as of 2010, responsible for determining 'major' applications within 13 or 16 weeks (depending upon the size and scale and whether a process known as an Environmental Impact Assessment is required). It is not uncommon for even quite minor applications to take weeks, months, maybe even years, before they can secure permission (if, indeed, they do at all). The speed at which planning applications were approved is shown in the table below:

Project	Submitted	Approved
New Marks & Spencer store	15 July 1997	18 September 1997
Shambles West retail development	6 August 1997	24 October 1997
The Printworks	8 September 1997	7 November 1997
Extension of Arndale Centre along Corporation Street frontage between Market Street & Cannon Street	9 January 1998	12th March 1998
Corn Exchange refurbishment and alterations	6 July 1998	10 September 1998
Creation of City Park (now known as Cathedral Gardens)	28 May 1999	8 July 1999

Delivering timescales as outlined above would simply not have been possible without Manchester City Council and Manchester Millennium working pro-actively with landowners and associated professionals with meetings and discussions taking place on a regular, sometimes daily, basis. This really was Manchester 'making it happen'. In 1999, the rebuilding project was awarded the 'Silver Jubilee Cup' by the Royal Town Planning Institute. This was an award devoted to the professionals that had delivered highly accomplished work, across the British Isles, not only in physical projects but also in planning processes, policy and plan-making. In an interview published by *Planning* magazine on 29 January 1999 Peter Babb, 'City Centre Group Leader' at Manchester City Council at the time, emphasised the importance of pre-application discussions and careful briefing behind the scenes:

'[they] helped enormously in getting major applications through in a short space of time.'

The developers working in Manchester agreed and had nothing but praise. In an interview published by *Property Week* on 29 October 1999 Lee Richardson, whose firm Richardson Developments was behind 'The Printworks', was complementary:

'They've been very, very helpful. I can't speak strongly enough for them. It's worked very well and we'd like other cities to be like this.'

In the same article Joe Malvisi of Frogmore Estates, then owners of the Corn Exchange, shared his enthusiasm:

'They've been tremendously helpful and had a very clear vision of what they've wanted to do. I can't think of another city with the dynamism of Manchester.'

WHAT HAPPENED NEXT ?

The post-bomb masterplan process, like the regeneration of Hulme, has become a template for schemes that have followed elsewhere in the city centre (both large and small). All the main elements were established and tested: close council and developer relations based on shared goals and trust; a tendering process to identify and select the most appropriate delivery partners; consultation with principal organisations such as landowners; and a willingness to deal quickly and efficiently with the formal decision-making processes (such as determining planning applications) on the understanding that the quality of the scheme must not be compromised.

This partnership approach is at the heart of the stories that follow. In delivering schemes the various links in the chain must hold together. This includes, to name but a few: council officers, the elected members who make decisions at Committee, the public, landowners, investors, developers, consultees appointed by the Government and, of course, the Government. Should one of the links in the chain become loose or break, then the trust may be lost and the project can fail. As outlined in the introduction, it has not all been plain sailing, and from time to time this has happened in the city centre.

The themes that illustrate the rebuilding of Manchester city centre following the bomb are: commercial, residential, historic, retail, leisure and space and connectivity. These have all consistently been priorities, and challenges, for Manchester City Council and have guided the evolution of the city centre. Moreover, they are themes that are valued by people. While each element is important in its own right, it is the sum of these parts that, most of the time, creates a successful city centre; a place where people want to be – a place where people choose to be. It is the overlap of these elements, and the interaction between them, that have guided and inspired the inspirational decisions that have been made in Manchester.

© Cityco (Manchester's City Centre Management Company)

Cityco, Piccadilly Partnership and Corridor Manchester

The ethos of partnership and improving the city centre was melded after the bomb with the introduction of the 'City Centre Management Company Limited', now known as 'Cityco'. This body is the principal and co-ordinating city-centre partnership and was incorporated in May 2000. It is a not-for-profit company limited by guarantee and with no shareholders and has always had a private-sector chairman and a board majority of non-council representatives (along with City Council Chief Executive Sir Howard Bernstein and Leader Sir Richard Leese on the board).

Cityco is responsible for maintaining a strategic overview of the economic performance of the city centre, promoting the city centre, and facilitating the presentation, management and maintenance of the city centre environment.

Other similar partnerships have since been created in Manchester, such as the Piccadilly Partnership, responsible for the Piccadilly area, and Corridor Manchester, responsible for promoting future economic growth and investment from St Peter's Square to Whitworth Park.

Manchester City Council

Overleaf: Masterplan – aerial image.
AECOM Design + Planning

▲ Left to right: 1 Spinningfields Square, 1 The Avenue and John Rylands Library.

'Back in 1992, the last one out of the city centre each evening switched off the lights.'

– *Estates Gazette*, 13 March 1999

COMMERCIAL

BEFORE THE BOMB

As outlined earlier in the book, Manchester had enjoyed years of economic opulence in the mid-to-late 19th century and early part of the 20th century, following through until World War Two. The years that followed were incredibly tough as industries collapsed and jobs were lost. An emerging trend that countered this decline was the growth of the financial and professional services sector – reflected by the construction of office buildings.

Many post-war office buildings in the city centre were speculative, uncoordinated, and located along streets such as Mosley Street and Fountain Street (hereafter referred to as the 'central business district' or CBD). The most notable post-war attempt to break the mould and shift the centre of gravity of the office market was the Bank of England's move in 1971 from their wonderful offices on King Street to the Portland Street end of Charlotte Street. For many years this was a location that could be described as 'off pitch', away from Manchester's commercial heart.

By the late 1980s and early 1990s Manchester was making progress. Employment in banking and finance grew by 18,400, or 24 per cent, between 1981 and 1987. Similarly, those employed in public administration increased by 31,000 in the same time period. In line with this, the completion of office developments in Manchester city centre grew due to high demand. In 1990, 715,400sq ft (66,500m²) was completed – double that in 1989. What was also noticeable was the expansion. During this time period only 62,000sq ft (5,800m²) of new development was in the traditional central business district. Manchester was making progress.

But the city still did not quite have the buzz of a vibrant commercial centre. People still needed to be convinced that Manchester city centre really was a genuine place to locate.

REBUILDING **MANCHESTER**

▶ New office schemes outside the traditional office core, 1990.

 Traditional Office Core

 New Office Schemes

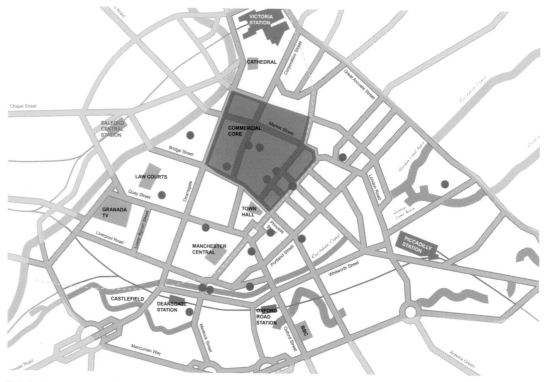

This feeling was captured by Rupert Barron of property consultants Chesterton in an interview with *Estates Gazette*, published on 13 March 1999:

'Back in 1992, the last one out of the city centre each evening switched off the lights.'

There was still a problem with the 'take up' of space in certain parts of the city. The area that would be devastated by the bomb on 15 June 1996 in a sense typified the standard of many office buildings in the city centre at the time: built post-war, of limited architectural value and suffering from low levels of demand. Despite being centrally located, the Shambles Square offices (of which there were three: Canon, Macintosh and Premier House) along with the Arndale Tower had proved unpopular with potential tenants. Similarly, owners of the Corn Exchange, Frogmore Estates, right up to the day of the blast, were offering low rents in an attempt to attract businesses to the area. A large banner stood aloft above the main entrance, announcing:

'Move in today! Low cost offices / storage to let from 100sq ft'

By the early 1990s the tide was slowly starting to turn. A number of new office schemes were delivered in the city centre, located outside the traditional CBD and thereby expanding the traditional office core. This included developments such as St James' House and 1 St James Square, along with Albion Wharf on Albion Street and Paradise Wharf on Ducie Street.

▼ The entrance to the Corn Exchange, 1995.

The work of the CMDC also helped with the completion of the eye-catching office development at 100 and 101 Barbirolli Square in 1996, designed by architects Renton Howard Wood Levin (RHWL). The quality of design was also improving radically with 82 King Street (overleaf), and shortly after The Observatory on Cross Street, designed by Holford Associates.

AFTER THE BOMB

Strangely, the impact of the bomb had a negligible impact on Manchester's office market. It led to the redistribution of businesses to alternative premises in the city centre (some temporary, some permanent). Royal Insurance, later known as Royal and Sun Alliance, moved southwards from their devastated Longridge House building to St George's House on Peter Street, while British Engine and CTEC (tenants of the same building) moved to Westminster House on Portland Street and Wellington House at Piccadilly Gardens.

In an article published in the August 1996 edition of *North West Insider* magazine, Martin Regan provided an explanation:

'…of the 620,000sq ft [of office space damaged by the blast] around half was empty and half of the remainder was let on mainly short term leases to very small businesses, the type that by definition are constantly ceasing to trade and being replaced. Therefore, the immediate economic impact has been the loss of the economic activity from around 150,000sq ft – yet all 620,000sq ft will need to be rebuilt.'

▲ Bank Chambers, Faulkner Street.

◄ The Observatory, Cross Street.

It was, however, a major opportunity to clear away many of these misplaced, isolated buildings and to build high-quality offices elsewhere in the city – something that would be more attractive to potential tenants. In turn the retail offering in this area could be strengthened considerably (one of the primary masterplan objectives).

It is important to remember that Manchester was, by this time, already making bold steps in terms of its recovery following years of economic decline. As a symbol of progress in 1997 the city was identified, for the first time, as one of the top 10 cities for business location in the Healey and Baker European Cities Monitor, beating cities such as Munich, Dusseldorf, Berlin and Dublin. The city was still behind – but now competing with – Milan, Zurich and Barcelona.

As work on the bomb-damaged area commenced, visions for new innovative business space elsewhere in the city centre were put in place. The city council would simply not rest. In his Proof of Evidence prepared for the Free Trade Hall public inquiry in April 1998 (see 'Historic' chapter), new Chief Executive Howard Bernstein outlined the vision:

'"Standing still" is not an option. To move to the top flight of international cities, Manchester must become a major destination city, despite its geographic peripherality in relation to Europe. To achieve this it must make best use of its assets and resources.'

© Euan Kellie

▶   82 King Street.

The outcome, in a commercial sense, has been the development of a series of 'hubs' across the city centre and its fringe – in turn, expanding the boundary of the city centre (certainly in terms of perception – very few people, apart from those working in the area, would have visited Crown Square pre-Spinningfields). A common theme has prevailed throughout: high quality and diverse buildings from respected local, national and international architects, the creation of excellent office space (typically Grade A – see definition) and an opportunity for new businesses to locate in Manchester city centre and create jobs. The 'Manchester Model' has appeared time and time again with close council and developer relations. None of this would have been possible without trust.

Two very distinct trends have emerged: The first of these can be described as 'comprehensive development areas' – similar in many ways to the approach adopted by the city council in the immediate post-war years. These areas are characterised by the size of the developments (both in terms of land, amount of financial investment, size of office floor space and the mix of activities). The second has been the continued fostering of small-scale, high-quality commercial developments across and within the city centre (sometimes filling in the few remaining pieces of vacant land – in many cases replacing obsolete post-war buildings which had no future) to complement, and balance, these major developments and provide diversity.

COMPREHENSIVE DEVELOPMENT AREAS

The comprehensive commercial developments in Manchester have all been characterised by the same processes: joint ventures between Manchester City Council and a series of property developers and investors. This way, opportunities have been unlocked in a way that benefits both parties and their respective interests. For the developers and investors, the provision of lettable floor space and an income stream; for the city council the attraction of small, medium and large businesses, creating job opportunities at all levels in different parts of the city centre.

The key ingredient that has enabled prompt delivery of each project is city council support from the earliest stages, on the proviso that the schemes meet the following criteria:

• Schemes are built.
• Deliver high-quality architecture.
• Enhance the environmental quality of the city.
• Integrate with the rest of the city.

This mechanism has worked time and time again. While it establishes a layer of support and a series of guiding principles, it also offers sufficient room for manoeuvre – something of huge importance bearing in mind the vulnerability and dynamic nature of the property market. From a developer's perspective it has meant that they can operate within a framework and start to deliver each element (by way of a planning application as a first step) as and when appropriate. This process typically has had a snowball effect, inspiring market confidence in a property sector and geographic location, unlocking finance and securing delivery. The city council in each and every case has asked for one commitment: trust.

Grade A offices

Office buildings within the 'Grade A' bracket are typically brand new or have been recently redeveloped, or experienced a thorough refurbishment. The properties are prestigious and usually occupy prime locations within major cities such as central London, Manchester and Birmingham.

Along with the standard of the building itself, Grade A offices will also possess high-quality furnishings, state-of-the-art facilities, and excellent accessibility. The property will be finished in order to compete for premier office users, typically appealing to an international market, and will usually demand rents that are above average for the area.

Offices can also be classed as Grade B and C.

▲ The proposed 'processional way' which would have connected the new Town Hall (centre of picture) with Crown Square – taken from the City of Manchester Plan 1945.

SPINNINGFIELDS

A major new vision for the city that would significantly alter the Manchester office market, the skyline, and also play a role in positioning the city within Europe's business elite was also taking shape before the bomb. The proposals that have emerged ironically focus upon one of the few areas of city centre land that had been implemented in accordance (in part) with the vision outlined in the City of Manchester Plan 1945. The initial vision was to create a 'processional way', thus linking Courts of Justice and Crown Square with Albert Square. This vision was softened somewhat and reappeared in the '1967 City Centre Map'. Here the council re-packaged the proposals as 'The Civic Area', one of five comprehensive proposals in the city centre at the time, and sought to create a business area 'for purposes connected with Government and Local Government'.

By the mid-1990s the area had been substantially redeveloped, with major new buildings for the Magistrates and the Crown Courts, the newspaper publishing complex on Deansgate and the College of Building. It included some older buildings – most notably the wonderful gothic John Rylands Library along Deansgate. Like the bomb-damaged area, it was marked by few active frontages and a number of low-rise post-war office buildings. Even the council's 1995 Unitary Development Plan recognised that the area was not of strategic importance and that it made no more than a 'modest contribution to the wider needs of the city centre.'

Nevertheless, the various landowners, which included property development and investment company Allied London, and Manchester City Council, had a bigger vision. In an interview published by the *Manchester Evening News* on 18 September 2007, CEO of Allied London Mike Ingall, who had joined the company in 1996, explained how they had in 1997 bought a number of buildings in the Crown Square area around the John Rylands Library, including Cumberland House (home to the city's register office) and the former home of the *Manchester Evening News*. The plan, initially, was to package the assets with some others and sell them on, making a profit of about £2 million along the way. His visit to the city centre in the summer of 1996 was the catalyst:

'I knew Manchester quite well – I'd tried to buy the Corn Exchange in 1993…As I arrived I saw Northcliffe House, which was empty, I saw the car park opposite on Hardman Street, and the big car parks further down past the Crown Court. I walked around the site and thought "this is huge".'

Discussions took place with the city council. It became clear very quickly that they shared a vision: replace and enhance many buildings and create a major new business quarter and destination. To allow this to happen the Manchester public/private partnership model was activated. Allied London formed the

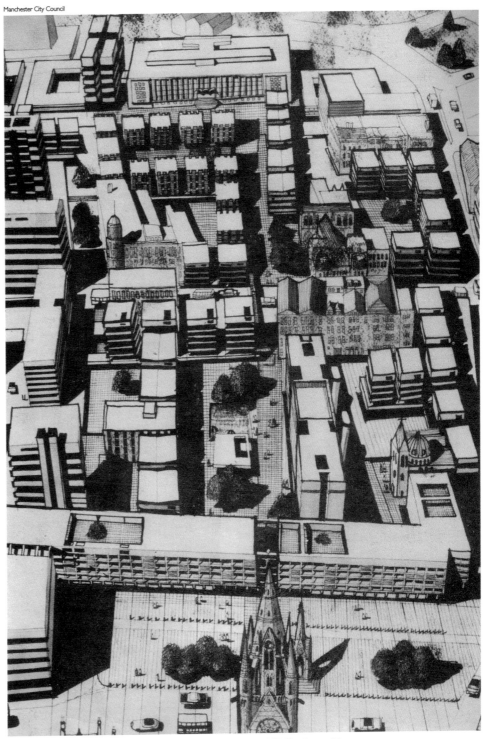

Manchester City Council

▲　A sketch showing the 'Civic Quarter' vision, taken from the 1967 City Centre Map.

79

REBUILDING **MANCHESTER**

▶ Spinningfields before redevelopment.

Spinningfields Development Group with Manchester City Council and Manchester College of Art & Technology (MANCAT), who also owned land nearby. When the vision was made public by Mike Ingall in 1997, branded tentatively at this time as the 'New Quarter', it was met by many with cynicism, particularly due to the size of the project and its unorthodox location away from the traditional established office zones of Fountain Street and King Street. He relayed his thoughts in an interview with *The Grid* magazine in May 2004:

'There was big-time scepticism as to how the scheme would work. When I began to discuss it with our professional team in 1997, people thought I'd flown in from Mars.'

Once again, like Hulme and the bomb-damaged core, a masterplan was developed for Spinningfields which outlined the vision and objectives. The city council endorsed the proposal with the formal 'adoption' of the masterplan in summer 2000, prepared by BDP. Now it really was time to deliver.

With a focus on high-quality design, Allied London carved up the site and appointed a host of first-class architects, including Foster + Partners, Denton Corker Marshall, Aedas AHR, Gensler, Renton Howard Wood Levine, Sheppard Robson and Skidmore, Owings & Merill. The title of 'New Quarter' was eventually replaced with the somewhat more catchy 'Spinningfields'. The name came from an 18th-century map of Manchester that recorded the weaving sheds located within the area during the city's days of cloth manufacturing.

▼ Absence of active frontages, pre-Spinningfields.

◄ An aerial shot of Spinningfields in the 1980s.

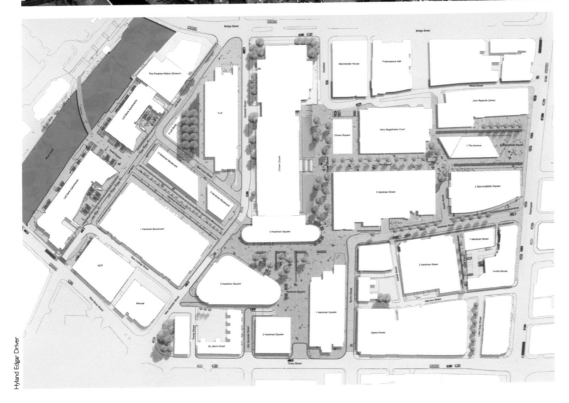

Hyland Edgar Driver

Stephen Welsh

▲▼ Spinningfields before and during redevelopment.

Stephen Welsh

◄ Spinningfields Masterplan.

81

For those who were not convinced by Spinningfields and felt that it would not happen, 2001 would mark a line in the sand:

Firstly, the Royal Bank of Scotland (RBS) signed up for almost 500,000sq ft (46,450m^2) of office space in two headquarter buildings at Spinningfields Square and Hardman Boulevard. This was, at the time, the biggest letting to a single user and the city's largest post-war leasing deal. To provide a comparison, the biggest letting deal at Canary Wharf in London was 1.5 million sq ft (140,000m^2) by Enron in 2000.

Secondly, Spinningfields was selected as the location for the Manchester Civil Justice Centre by Her Majesty's Court Service.

In terms of timing, Spinningfields hit the track at absolutely the right time. Even though Manchester's office market was getting stronger in the late 1990s, with more and more businesses 'taking up space' and choosing to locate in the city centre, commentators were concerned that there were not enough new buildings 'in the pipeline' to accommodate such demand and, consequently, businesses would locate outside of Manchester. With hindsight they need not have worried. Planning permissions for individual plots at Spinningfields started to roll in and work on site commenced promptly, mainly with the demolition of buildings.

Stephen Welsh

▶ Demolition of the old Magistrates Court at Spinningfields .

▲ Spinningfields under construction.

Heritage matters would appear on the radar early on as planning permission was sought in 2001 to demolish Northcliffe House and the YHA building which fronted onto Deansgate and fell within the Deansgate and Peter Street conservation area. They were also close to listed buildings such as John Rylands Library (Grade I) and the County Court (Grade II). This is described in greater detail in the 'Historic' chapter.

Notwithstanding, planning permission was granted. Nothing now was going to stand in the way of delivery. From 2002 onwards Spinningfields, along with 'Leftbank', turned into a huge building site.

REBUILDING **MANCHESTER**

▲ The changing face of Manchester – looking towards the city centre and Spinningfields in 2000, 2005 and 2006.

Spinningfields Development Pipeline

Spring 2002 — Manchester College of Arts and Technology opens.

Spring 2004 — Magistrates Court is completed. 1 Spinningfields Square, The Royal Bank of Scotland's NW Regional Headquarters, designed by architects Sheppard Robson and RHWL, is completed.

Summer 2004 — 1 Hardman Boulevard, designed by architects RHWL, is completed.

Spring 2005 — Work starts on 2 Hardman Street, designed by architects BDP, and 3 and 4 Hardman Square, designed by Foster + Partners.

Summer 2005 — First new retailers at Spinningfields, Wagamama and Eat commence trading.

Spring 2006 — 3 Hardman Street, designed by Sheppard Robson is completed and pre-let to Guardian Media Group and Deloitte.

Summer 2006 — 685-space multi-storey NCP car park, designed by architects Carey Jones, is completed.

Autumn 2006 — Construction begins on 3 Hardman Street, designed by Sheppard Robson.

Spring 2007 — 3 and 4 Hardman Square are completed and pre-let to Halliwells, HSBC and Grant Thornton.

Summer 2007 — The Civil Justice Centre, designed by Denton Corker Marshall, is completed.

Autumn 2007 — Work begins on No 1 The Avenue, designed by Sheppard Robson.

Spring 2008 — Work begins on The People's History Museum exterior and 1 Crown Square, designed by architects Gensler.

Spinningfields will, once complete, represent an investment of £1.5 billion and have delivered the following on the 30-acre site:

- 4.6 million sq ft (430,000 m²) of commercial, civic, residential, retail and open space.
- 6 acres of public realm.
- 20 signature new buildings.
- 5 new public squares.
- 2.37 million sq ft (220,180m²) of class A office space.
- 300,000sq ft (27,800m²) of complementary high-end retail and leisure areas.
- 391 luxury apartments in the Leftbank complex.
- 685-space NCP Car Park.
- 3 BREEAM Excellent ratings for the Civil Justice Centre, 1 The Avenue and 3 Hardman Street.
- 350,000sq ft (32,500m²) at 3 Hardman Street – one of the largest office buildings in the UK.
- 25,000 office workers occupying the site when fully occupied.

Some of the notable businesses that have chosen to locate at Spinningfields include Halliwells, Regus, Barclays Bank, Marks & Spencer, Beachcrofts, the Ministry of Justice, the General Medical Council and the Guardian Media Group. Restaurants include Carluccio's, Wagamama, Samsi, Giraffe, Strada, Zizzi, Eat, Bagel Nash, Pret A Manger GBK, Nando's and Bar Ha Ha.

▲ 3 Hardman Square.

▶ I The Avenue.

▼ I Spinningfields Square.

It is impossible to not draw attention to some of Spinningfields' awards. Here is a quick sample:

- Developer of the Year for Spinningfields – Property Week Offices 2009 Awards.
- Civic Trust Award for Sustainability and The Civil Justice Centre – Civic Trust Awards 2009.
- Commercial Developer of the Year – The Northwest Property Awards 2008.
- RIBA Sustainability Award for The Civil Justice Centre – RIBA Awards 2008

Above all else, it is a wonderful example of the partnership approach advocated by Manchester City Council and what it can deliver.

© Aidan O'Rourke - www.aidan.co.uk

Commission Air

▲ Aerial image – Spinningfields.

Civil Justice Centre

Summer 2007 saw the completion of one of Manchester city centre's finest buildings: the Civil Justice Centre. In 2002, Her Majesty's Courts Service held an international competition to select an architect to design new purpose-built premises for the Department of Justice in the North West, the biggest court complex to be built in the UK since the Royal Courts of Justice opened in London in 1882. The building was procured through the UK's Public Private Partnership model. The decision-making process was revolutionary: the Lord Chancellor's Department would choose the designer independently of site and developer. Following the selection of Spinningfields as the chosen location for the centre, an international design competition was held, attracting submissions from over 50 teams across the globe. The award of the project eventually went to architects Denton Corker Marshall.

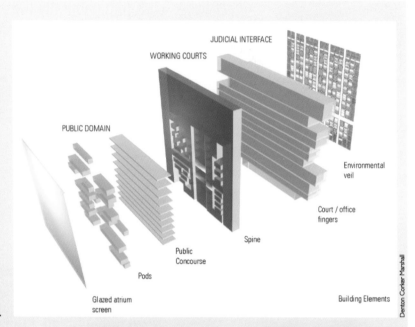

▶   Civil Justice Centre building elements.

▲   A sketch of the Civil Justice Centre, designed by architects Denton Corker Marshall.

▲   The proposed interior of the Civil Justice Centre.

Following selection and the due planning process, permission was granted by Manchester City Council on 20 March 2003 (determined in less than nine weeks). Delivery was prompt. The site on Gartside Street, which was previously occupied by a multi-storey car park adjacent to the Courts of Justice, was cleared and in early 2004 a groundbreaking ceremony was held. Thirteen months later, in July 2005, the Civil Justice Centre was 'topped out'.

▲ The Civil Justice Centre, under construction.

▲ The Civil Justice Centre.

The building was officially opened by Her Majesty Queen Elizabeth II on 28 February 2008 and is the largest court development to be built in Britain for 125 years. Standing next to the Crown Courts and visible from the Town Hall, the Civil Justice Centre finally fulfils the promise of a fitting centrepiece for Manchester's legal quarter, as envisioned in the 1945 Plan for Manchester.

The building provides 47 court or hearing rooms, 75 consultation rooms, office and support areas within a landmark 16-storey, 350,000sq ft (34,000m^2), £160 million development. By 2010 the building had won over 20 national and international awards for construction, engineering, environmental sustainability and architecture, including being shortlisted for the RIBA prestigious Stirling Prize 2008.

In Manchester it is held in the highest esteem, not least of all by Leader Sir Richard Leese, as outlined in his *Leaders Blog* on 28 February 2008:

'This is exactly the sort of building that helps instil pride in our city, and reinforces our history of original and modern achievements. It is already award-winning and I'm sure there will be many architectural awards to come for this classy addition to Manchester's portfolio and unlike many award winning buildings I don't think this one will go pear-shaped in a few years.'

◄ Manchester Civil Justice Centre.

PICCADILLY PLACE

The second comprehensive development area is that of Piccadilly Place, located across the road from Piccadilly Station. It would form part of the council's wider vision for the Piccadilly area, known as the 'Piccadilly Gateway'.

For many years the site had been a regeneration priority for the city council, forming part of a wider initiative for the Piccadilly Gateway. It was run down, provided only surface car parking, some landscaping and little physical connectivity with Piccadilly Station (or the rest of the surrounding area for that matter). Its main attraction was the delights of the Piccadilly Indian Tandoori, which was hardly a fitting sight to greet visitors to the city. Having acquired the land, Manchester City Council and the Greater Manchester Passenger Transport Executive (GMPTE) prioritised the regeneration and redevelopment of the site. A development partner was still needed to help bring a scheme forward, though. Akin to the bomb masterplan, it was time for a competition so that the most appropriate partner could be identified and selected. In February 2002, London-based property developers Argent were selected ahead of a joint venture proposed by Amec Construction and Crosby Homes to work in partnership with the city council and GMPTE and lead the redevelopment.

Founded in 1981, Argent had become a leading practitioner of city-centre regeneration. Led by joint CEOs David Partridge and Roger Madelin their impressive back catalogue of developments includes the Brindleyplace scheme in Birmingham, and they had just been chosen to take forward King's Cross Central – one of the most significant developments in central London.

▶ Piccadilly Place, before redevelopment.

© Aidan O'Rourke - www.aidan.co.uk

Argent Estates Limited

The subsequent vision for the site was to create a high-quality, mixed-use development that would dramatically improve the area and become a destination in its own right. David Partridge, speaking to magazine *The Grid* in April 2004, made it clear that a key objective was to change people's perceptions about an area which had traditionally been seen as somewhere for 'chip butties and cans of lager'.

Following their selection as development partner, and as a further commitment to the delivery of high-quality architecture, Argent went on to hold their own design competition – this time to select architects for the Piccadilly Place masterplan, which would set the framework for the site and the individual proposals that would follow. London-based architects Clarke Associates were initially selected but went on to be replaced by Austin-Smith:Lord. Their vision was to subdivide what would become known as 'Piccadilly Place' into distinct elements, providing a hotel, high-quality office buildings, a piazza and a bridge across London Road, thereby providing connectivity with Piccadilly Station and enhancing the pedestrian experience.

The framework, which sought to provide a 'comprehensive, phased, mixed-use development' at Piccadilly Place, was endorsed by Manchester City Council on 29 May 2003. This would enable the delivery, piece by piece, of the various elements – exactly the same process as that adopted after the bomb.

The ethos of project tendering and high-quality design continued rapidly in the months that followed. Argent held a public competition to choose a 'Poem for Manchester' – which is proudly displayed in the new piazza – and went on to hold another design competition in October 2003; this time, to choose individual architects for each phase of Piccadilly Place. The following list introduces the architects that went on to be selected by Argent in May 2004 and the buildings and spaces they went on to deliver.

One Piccadilly Place	Mark Weintraub Associates	Home to the 285-bed City Inn hotel.
Two Piccadilly Place	Weedon Partnership Architects	New 55,000sq ft (5,110m²) headquarters for the GMPTE.
Three Piccadilly Place	Austin-Smith:Lord	200,000sq ft (19,000m²) of office accommodation.
Four Piccadilly Place	Hodder Associates	125,000sq ft (11,600m²) of office accommodation.
Five Piccadilly Place (also known as 'The Hub')	Glen Howells Architects	167 studio, one, two and three bed apartments.
Manchester Curve	Wilkinson Eyre	New pedestrian bridge which links Piccadilly Place to Manchester Piccadilly Station. It was named by the people of Manchester.

Planning applications for the individual buildings and spaces at Piccadilly Place were prepared, submitted and dealt with promptly by the city council. This reflected the extensive, ongoing pre-planning application discussions between the city council, Argent and their associated architects. Equally, the various elements were delivered – a continued demonstration of the trust shared between all parties in the process.

The turnaround was remarkable. At the beginning of 2004 the site was still a grubby hot-bed of criminal activity, with little more than short-stay car parks. By 2010:

- The majority of Piccadilly Place was complete.
- Many of the units were occupied, including tenants such as the GMPTE in Two Piccadilly Place.
- As an indicator of the design quality, Three Piccadilly Place secured two awards in 2007: the Manchester Chamber of Commerce and Industry 'Building of the Year' awards and the Property Week 'Green Building Award'.

David Partridge is very clear about what makes Manchester a great place in which to invest:

'With Manchester, the more you put in the more you get out. It is a city that thrives off partnerships and looking beyond the bottom line.'

Hodder + Partners

Argent Estates Limited

▲ Four Piccadilly Place.

▲ Two Piccadilly Place.

▼ Three Piccadilly Place.

Austin-Smith:Lord

▲   One Piccadilly Place, designed by Weintraub Associates.

▲   Five Piccadilly Place.

▼   Manchester Curve, Piccadilly Place, designed by Wilkinson Eyre.

▲   One, Two and Three Piccadilly Place under construction.

▲ Three Piccadilly Place under construction.

Argent Estates Limited

◄ Piccadilly Place under construction.

PICCADILLY BASIN

The regeneration of the Piccadilly Basin had, like Piccadilly Place, been a council priority for many years, also forming part of the wider 'Piccadilly Gateway' initiative.

What makes this comprehensive development particularly interesting is the speed of delivery – a complete contrast to the high-octane Spinningfields. Landowners Town Centre Securities, a property investment and development company founded in 1959, have played a very steady, long-term game with Piccadilly Basin by choosing to build schemes as and when an occupant or 'end user' comes forward. This approach has been quite different to developments elsewhere in the city, where commercial projects have been delivered on a speculative basis (and therefore at higher risk).

▼ Aerial shot of Piccadilly Basin, 2008.

Town Centre Securities

Located behind Piccadilly Station, the vision for the Basin is captured by Town Centre Securities' promotional brochure:

'This sought-after urban oasis offers a mix of office, residential, retail and leisure accommodation with some 750 multi-storey car parking spaces planned in an idyllic setting. The newly refurbished canals converge at the hub of the scheme and the picturesque marina, riverside walkways, landscaped areas and wildlife within Piccadilly Basin ensure that all residents, tenants and visitors get the very best of urban life.'

While Piccadilly Basin has been delivered at different pace to that of Spinningfields, the delivery process has, however, been the same:

- A vision for the area, supported in principle by the city council.
- Preparation of a masterplan (prepared by Ian Simpson Architects in 1997).
- Approved and supported by the council (granted in August 1998).
- Delivery by different architects, piece by piece.

The elements of the Basin that have so far been delivered are:

Carver's Warehouse	Ian Simpson Architects	A sensitively restored refurbished office building providing 24,000sq ft (2,300m²) of space.
11 Ducie Street	BDP	The five-storey building provides 33,000sq ft (3,065m²) of office space.
Jackson's Warehouse	Michael Hyde & Associates	A converted listed building with 40 apartments and duplexes, along with a ground-floor bar/restaurant.
Vantage Quay	Conran & Partners	Over 100 one and two-bed apartments, over seven floors.
Car Park	Ian Simpson Architects	Completed in January 2006 with parking for 242 cars.
Landmark Retail Unit	Schmidt, Hammer & Lassen	The 141,000sq ft (14,000m²) scheme was completed in August 2006 and was originally home to furniture store Ilva.

There is still much more to come at Piccadilly Basin, not least of all the refurbished Brownsfield Mill, located off Great Ancoats Street. With major strategic schemes such as New Islington and Ancoats Urban Village across the road, it will be an area to watch closely over the next decade.

▼ Carver's Warehouse: before redevelopment.

▼ Carver's Warehouse: after redevelopment (interior).

▼ Carver's Warehouse: after redevelopment (exterior).

Town Centre Securities

▲   11 Ducie Street, Piccadilly
Basin.

▶   11 Ducie Street, Piccadilly
Basin.

Town Centre Securities

▲ Jackson's Warehouse, Piccadilly Basin.

REBUILDING **MANCHESTER**

▶ Vantage Quay, Piccadilly Basin.

© Euan Kellie

Town Centre Securities

▶ Car Park, Piccadilly Basin.

◀ Ilva (now Aldi), Piccadilly Basin.

© Euan Kellie

Town Centre Securities

◀ Brownsfield Mill, Piccadilly Basin.

▲   Aerial image of Gaythorn Gas Works, 1930.

FIRST STREET

In December 2000 the 'Southern Gateway', an area lying south of the core of the city centre between Oxford Road and Chester Road, was endorsed by Manchester City Council's Executive Department as a strategic priority for comprehensive regeneration, with a focus on large-scale office developments. Architect Sir Terry Farrell was appointed by the city council in February 2002 to prepare a framework for the area; the objective being to encourage landmark development that would enhance the city's competitiveness 'on a global scale', attracting indigenous and inward investment and providing new employment opportunities.

A key part of the Southern Gateway was a sub-area known as 'Central Spine' (so called because of Albion Street, which provides a link to the motorway network and Manchester Airport). This comprised some 20 acres of predominantly under-utilised land and premises, including an area known as 'Grand Island', previously occupied by the Gaythorn Gasworks and now home to the former British Council building, occupied by British Telecom up until 2006. It was clear that the area had great potential due to its location, although it had suffered from a lack of identity and economic purpose resulting from its failure to integrate and connect physically and economically with the rest of the city centre and the adjacent Hulme and City South area.

In September 2005, Manchester City Council and the North West Development Agency invited the BBC – who at the time, were considering plans to relocate to the Manchester City region – to become the anchor tenant of a Media Enterprise Zone in Manchester city centre; more specifically, Central Spine. As a first delivery phase a detailed Development Framework was prepared in November 2005, which aimed to set a bold new vision for the area as a vibrant and diverse new gateway entrance to Manchester. This, in turn, would facilitate a natural and seamless expansion of the city centre.

In January 2006 two sites were shortlisted by the BBC: Central Spine and Pier 9 at Salford Quays. Final bids were submitted by both parties in April. Following evaluation, the BBC announced in June 2006 that they were entering a period of exclusive discussion with Salford with a view to making them the preferred bidder. Shortly after, Salford was confirmed as the final location.

Manchester's bid team was disappointed – not least of all the city council. In an interview published by the *Evening News* on 29 August 2006, BBC North Project Director Mark Thomas explained that he was not surprised:

▲ Visualisation of First Street.

▲ Visualisation of First Street proposals.

▲ Grand Island Building, First Street.

107

'You only have to look around at what's been achieved in Manchester to acknowledge that neither Sir Howard Bernstein, nor Richard Leese, are used to losing. Therefore, this probably came as an unpleasant surprise.'

They may not be used to losing, but they are familiar with setbacks and how to respond. This was no different.

Once the dust had settled, the city council focused on reigniting the Central Spine vision. During 2007 and 2008 the original Development Framework was 'refreshed' by the city council. During this time a significant change of ownership had taken place across the site with the acquisition by Ask Developments of all the land and buildings previously owned by Henderson Global Investors (predominantly the Grand Island building, previously occupied by BT). A new masterplan was prepared by architects Michael Squire and Partners; the guiding principles remained valid: create a dynamic business environment in engaging and stimulating landscaped surroundings.

In 2008 Central Spine was rebranded as 'First Street'. The updated Development Framework went on to identify the delivery of over 3.2 million sq ft (280,000m²) of new and refurbished commercial, residential, retail and leisure floorspace – almost half of this would be office space.

With the framework in place, land and buildings were prepared for occupation at First Street between late 2008 and 2009. The first key phase that was complete by the end of 2009 was that of the substantial refurbishment of the Grand Island office building (retitled Number One First Street). It was also announced in May 2009 that the city council had chosen to temporarily occupy 140,000sq ft (13,000m²) of space within the building while the town hall complex is refurbished.

As First Street is delivered over the coming years it will undoubtedly become an exciting part of the city, with high-quality buildings and landscaped space, providing a vital strategic link with the rest of the city-centre fringe.

▼　First Street signage, City Road East.

▲ Commercial Core Strategy – Priority Area.

COMMERCIAL CORE

As projects such as Spinningfields gathered pace in the early years of the new millennium, it became clear that some existing city-centre office occupiers would choose to move from older buildings elsewhere in the city into the modern Grade A office accommodation. The RBS and NatWest alone occupied 23 buildings in various parts of the city centre. While this was good news, it meant that, slowly but surely, the CBD was losing its edge. *Property Week* on 5 March 2004 drew attention to its perceived decline, characterised by Mosley Street:

'The road is neglected and punctuated by intermittent clutter of street trams, while the decaying hulk of Eagle Star House provides and unwelcome blemish on a modern city centre seeking inward investment.'

Manchester City Council quickly placed an emphasis upon unlocking opportunities within the established central business district. Just like the comprehensive development areas, it was time to introduce the magic formula:

* A clear vision and framework.
* Delivery of high-quality buildings and spaces.
* Partnership.

At the city council's Executive Committee on 19 March 2003 the 'Commercial Core Strategy' was presented. The area was broadly defined by Cross Street, Princess Street, Mosley Street and land to the rear of Market Street. A series of buildings and zones was identified by the strategy, including: Eagle Star House on Mosley Street; Amethyst House on Brown Street; Cheshire, Derby, Cooper House on Booth Street/Brown Street and Princess Street/Kennedy Street.

The vision was clear:

'A number of sites have been identified which have the greatest potential for redevelopment. These are buildings which were constructed mainly in the 1960s/1970s and have come to the end of their useful life. They have all been the subject of discussions between officers and landowners/agents about their future redevelopment and some have detailed planning permission in place. They are also considered to pose some of the greatest environmental problems in the area and in these terms their redevelopment would be greatly beneficial. Officers believe that the commercial core would benefit greatly from the phased redevelopment of these sites and that the city council should work closely with owners and developers to assist in this process.'

With this framework in place, the CBD saw phenomenal development between 2003 and 2008. The following provides a sample of some of the schemes that were successfully delivered.

58 Mosley Street

By 2004 Eagle Star House had been empty for more than a decade and dominated the western side of Mosley Street. It was sold by owners Royal London Asset Management to Maple Grove, who went on to secure planning permission

Sheppard Robson

▲ Demolition of Eagle Star House, Mosley Street.

◀ 58 Mosley Street, designed by Sheppard Robson.

for a 105,000sq ft office building (9,755m²), designed by architects Sheppard Robson, with law firm Cobbetts taking up office space. Demolition commenced in mid-2004, and the site was clear by the beginning of 2005. The new building was complete at the end of 2006.

40 Spring Gardens

Langtree Developments were granted permission in 2004 to demolish Amethyst House, a vacant five-storey office block. In doing so they delivered 100,000sq ft (9,290m^2) of new Grade A office space at 40 Spring Gardens, designed by architects Aedas. Between November 2004 and May 2005 the site was cleared and replaced with 101,024sq ft (9,385m^2), almost half of which was pre-let to HBOS.

◀ The demolition of Amethyst House, Spring Gardens.

▶ 40 Spring Gardens.

▲ Cooper House.

▲ Derby House.

▲▼ The demolition of Derby House.

Jeremy Wolstencroft / George Steel

▲ The cleared Derby House and Cooper House site.

'Belvedere'

The third site involved Cheshire, Derby and Cooper House on Booth and Brown Street. There was a basement car park beneath all blocks and two live network sub-stations that had to remain live throughout the demolition works. Owned by Wilson Bowden Developments Limited, the site was cleared between June 2006 and January 2007 and replaced with 'Belvedere', 107,537sq ft (9,990m^2) of speculative development designed by Aedas.

► Belvedere, Booth Street.

© Euan Kellie

© Euan Kellie

▲ Chancery Place.

© Euan Kellie

▲ Scottish Provident House, 1996.

© Euan Kellie

▲ Scottish Provident House, October 2004.

Chancery Place

Located on a triangular site within the Upper King Street conservation area, surrounded by high-quality buildings and bound by Booth Street and Brown Street, Scottish Provident House had been vacant for a decade and had begun to attract social problems. In 2004 permission was secured to demolish the building, and work commenced on site shortly after; by the summer of 2005 the site was clear. A planning application was submitted by HKR Architects in October 2006 for the erection of a 15-story building with 80,000sq ft (7,432m^2) of office space with car parking and a mix of uses at ground floor. The application was approved in December 2006, and construction on site began in 2007. The scheme was completed in the second half of 2008.

© Euan Kellie

▶ Chancery Place site following demolition, 2007.

▼ Demolition of Scottish Provident House, May 2005.

© Euan Kellie

© Aidan O'Rourke - www.aidan.co.uk

Stephen Welsh

▲   80 Mosley Street (before).

80 Mosley Street

In May 2005 Robinson Architects secured permission
to alter and reclad the elevation of 80 Mosley Street.
By 2007 the project was complete, and lettings were
secured in early 2010.

◀   80 Mosley Street (after).

Bruntwood

Bruntwood are one of the largest commercial property companies in the UK and have, since the 1970s, focused on making the best use of existing assets. It is a family business, founded by current chairman Michael Oglesby and run by his son Chris, who became CEO in 2000.

By 2010 they own 90 office properties across Manchester, Leeds, Liverpool and Birmingham. This includes 62 properties in Manchester, equating to 4.3 million square feet.

Their contribution to the commercial office stock in Manchester city centre is unprecedented, with estimates suggesting they own 20 per cent of the market. Over the years they have retained and refurbished many post-war buildings that could quite easily have simply been demolished. The Piccadilly Plaza case study is of particular merit, as is the wonderful work along New York Street, with a selection of refurbished buildings such as 'The Exchange', 5 New York Street and Bank Chambers. This has been complemented with excellent new buildings such as 1 New York Street, designed by architects Denton Corker Marshall.

What is also of particular merit is the location mix. While most of their buildings can be found in the heart of the central business district, there are also properties in less salubrious locations such as 'Square One' on Travis Street to the rear of Piccadilly Station, delightfully and sensitively refurbished by architects Stephenson Bell.

As well as focusing on the fabric of the city by recycling buildings, Bruntwood play a part in the life and future of Manchester. Examples include:

- Each year they donate 10 per cent of profits to arts, civic and charitable causes.

- They are a founding sponsor of Manchester International Festival and have supported it through its growth.

- In 2002 they were one of the first companies to sign up as sponsors for The Commonwealth Games, helping to put Manchester on the world stage.

- To encourage and uncover new writing talent they have developed a nationally renowned playwriting competition, The Bruntwood Playwriting Competition with the Royal Exchange Theatre. To date they have received over 3,000 scripts and forged playwriting careers for six winners.

- In September 2010 they will reach their target of raising £500,000 for the Royal Manchester Children's Hospital, thus meeting a five-year objective.

- The Oglesby Charitable Trust provides grants to a broad spectrum of smaller charitable causes and has an income of approximately £750,000 per annum. Since 2000, the Trust has made grants in the region of £3,500,000.

- In 2008 they rescued Afflecks Palace when it was at risk of closing. Bruntwood now run the venture as 'Afflecks' and, in 2010, are undertaking work to restore the building whilst keeping its eclectic characteristics. Afflecks supports local artists and students by giving them an opportunity to showcase their work and is now fully occupied with a waiting list for stalls.

- They partnered with the University of Manchester on Eco Cities, a climate change adaptation project that will produce a climate change adaptation blueprint for the city of Manchester.

REBUILDING **MANCHESTER**

▲ I New York Street.

◄ New York Street.

▶ Square One, Travis Street.

CONCLUSION

In summing up, Manchester City Council has acted, in each case, as an enabler and a partner in each of these major commercial developments. The flexible framework and masterplan approach has given commitment, in principle, to the vision on each of the sites, while allowing the developers and investors to bring forward each piece in accordance with existing and future market conditions. This has allowed the city centre to expand, introduce new employment opportunities while delivering high-quality architecture reflected by strong levels of office 'take up' as illustrated by the graph. This model has also worked at the smaller scale, within the existing established city centre commercial core.

But also, as introduced earlier, the other side of the partnership is delivery from the private sector – the developers and investors who have financed the initiatives, the architects who have designed the buildings and the many professionals who have played a vital role in bringing the schemes forward. The future will certainly be exciting as further schemes come to fruition outside the existing city-centre boundary.

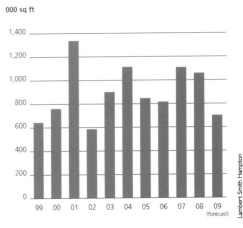

000 sq ft

▲   Manchester City Centre office market take up 1999-2009.

▼   View towards Manchester's commercial core.

▲   Box Works.

'Manchester is poised. Something is coming. It feels very exciting.

Let's see what happens with all these buildings, all these lofts.

There is going to be a real explosion in 2003 and 2004 when the

centre of Manchester is really lived in like no other city.'

– Anthony H. Wilson

RESIDENTIAL

BEFORE THE BOMB

The population of Manchester and the city centre has changed greatly over the years. During the 19th century, in line with the city's significant economic growth, a large proportion of Manchester's residents lived in, or close to, the city centre. Midway through this century, residents gradually moved out of the city as the railway system grew, as did the presence of warehouses. Consequently, land was gobbled up and the residential stock began to fall.

It was not until after World War Two that key stakeholders in Manchester started to give thought to the concept of modern city-centre living. If nothing else it would, at least, play a role in arresting the growth of suburbanisation which seemed to be steadily killing the city centre. Nicholas was silent on the topic in his 1945 Plan. One of the earliest references to post-war residential regeneration in the city that can be found dates back to 27 November 1959. It was reported by the *Manchester Guardian* that at the opening of the office building Longridge House on Corporation Street the Lord Mayor of Manchester, Alderman Quinney, appealed to architects to consider the possibility of using the top floors of new commercial buildings as flats. It was his belief that there was a

'…real need for dwelling places in central Manchester, and that small flats at the top of large office blocks would serve a valuable social purpose.'

While the idea was great on paper, it was no more than a pipe dream. The city-centre population was haemorrhaging. By 1961 it had fallen to 4,000 people. Ten years later it had crashed to only 200. Clearly, there was much to do.

The pulse of city-centre living started to beat with the introduction of the 1967 City Centre Map. Here it was seen as a concept that would not only help reverse the growing trend of suburbanisation but could also reduce travel and bring

REBUILDING **MANCHESTER**

life and vibrancy back into the area at all hours. A simple plan was included which identified three areas where residential development may be acceptable: Byrom Street, Smithfield and the Rochdale Canal. The 1967 City Centre Map pulled no punches, however, and recognised that the quality of the existing properties was largely dire:

'Only the Lord Byrom Street area may be identified as remotely residential in character. Even in this area, apart from the fine and well cared for Georgian town houses on John Street occupied in the main by medical consultants and professional offices, most of the remaining accommodation is sub-standard and much of it is subject to clearance proposals.'

THE FIRST PHASE

It was during the 1970s that the first true examples of post-war city-centre living in Manchester began to emerge. This included:

© Euan Kellie

▲ Cromford Court apartments, Arndale Centre.

▼ St John's Gardens.

© Euan Kellie

- St John's Gardens, unveiled by developer George Wimpey in 1979 on land owned by Manchester City Council within Castlefield. The scheme included 172 units, broken into four truly suburban-esque pieces: Culvercliff Walk, Ashill Walk, Porchfield Square and Rozel Square.

- The Arndale Centre curiously included 60 flats and maisonettes above the shops in the northern part of the development near Shudehill. The scheme was known as Cromford Court and was operated by Northern Counties Housing Association.

- The former Smithfield Market site in the Northern Quarter was developed in a phased manner by Manchester City Council on behalf of the council's Housing Committee, delivering 116 units.

Moving into the 1980s, there were three schemes in the city centre, and the council continued to promote the concept of city-centre living, demonstrated by the 1984 City Centre Local Plan:

'More recently…there has been the re-emergence of housing in the City Centre which, far from being simply an alternative to traditional uses, has a great deal to commend it. Whilst progress has not been as rapid or widespread as might have been hoped, those housing schemes which have been implemented at St. John's Gardens, Smithfield and in the Arndale Centre, have not only confirmed that housing is desirable, but also that it can be easily achieved.''

RESIDENTIAL

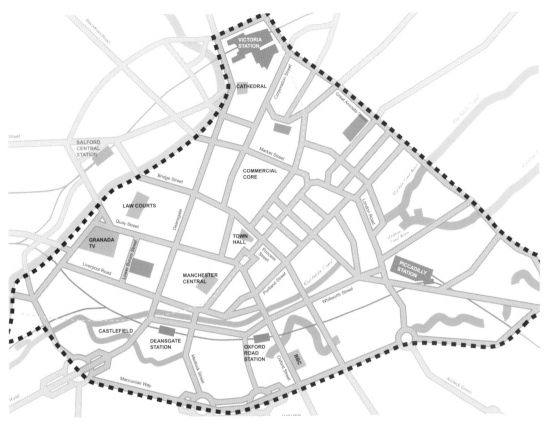

◀ Residential schemes in Manchester city centre, 1984.

City Centre Boundary

Existing housing

It was during this decade that people and processes truly came together in Manchester – sprinkled of course with entrepreneurialism and the new *modus operandi* adopted by the city council. Throw all of these factors, along with multiple derelict buildings, into the pot, and the output is innovative city-centre living. Manchester has become a place where people where people want to live; a place where it is fashionable to live.

Who was responsible and what was delivered?

First and foremost, it is important to acknowledge the work of local businessman and Salford bookmaker Jim Ramsbottom and his company Castlefield Estates. He acquired a portfolio of buildings in Castlefield, around the time of the conservation area designation in 1979. It was his firm belief that there was a market for these buildings which would be ideal for new media and design industries that were starting to establish in Manchester. This planted the seed for the creation of the Castlefield community and the considerable investment that would follow. Several significant development projects were delivered by Ramsbottom's company, in partnership with local architects. This included Eastgate (formerly Gail House) by Stephenson Somerville Bell, Merchants Warehouse by Simpson Associates and Dukes 92 by Stephenson, Somerville, Bell and OMI Architects. Funding from the CMDC also played a role in the delivery of these schemes.

▼ Derelict Merchants Warehouse.

123

REBUILDING **MANCHESTER**

▲   Merchants Warehouse, Castlefield, 1986.

▶   Merchants Warehouse, redesigned by Simpson Associates.

▼   Eastgate (formerly Gail House).

◀ Orient House, Granby Street.

The second was the Manchester Phoenix Initiative, which was set up in 1987. This was a non-profit-making organisation that sought to act as a catalyst for the regeneration of the city centre. It was, without doubt, an early indication of the public-private partnership approach that was starting to emerge. The Whitworth Street corridor, extending from Piccadilly westwards through to Castlefield, was the first project for the Initiative in early 1987. By 1991 the city-centre population had increased to 900, but this was just the beginning.

CONVERSIONS AND NEW BUILD

During the late 1980s and early 1990s city-centre living really gathered momentum. A major scheme that was under construction by the beginning of 1992 was that of Granby Village on Whitworth Street. This scheme involved the refurbishment of three Victorian buildings on Whitworth Street, Sackville Street and Granby Row and the construction of two six-storey buildings, Venice Court and Velvet Court. The £10.8 million development by Wimpey Homes would provide 211 flats for sale, along with a bar and restaurant.

▼ Bombay House, Whitworth Street.

▲ Velvet House, Bombay Street.

By the beginning of 1994, more and more residential developments had appeared in Manchester city centre. This included:

Scheme/Building	Street	Total no. of Units	Former Use	Developer
St John's Gardens		196	Vacant Land	Wimpey
Granby House	Granby Row	60	Warehouse	BP Construction
Chepstow House	Chepstow Street	88	Warehouse and Offices	Unknown
33	Faulkner Street	33	Warehouse and Offices	Tung Sing Housing Association
India House	Whitworth Street	140	Warehouse and Offices	Northern Counties Housing Association
Lancaster House	Whitworth Street	71	Warehouse and Offices	Housing Projects
Cromford Court	Arndale Centre	43	Vacant Land	Housing Association
Altrincham Terrace	Lower Albion Street	166	Vacant Land	UMIST
Bombay House	Whitworth Street	50	Warehouse and Offices	Wimpey
Velvet Court	Granby Row	58	Warehouse and Offices	Wimpey
57-59	Whitworth Street	39	Warehouse and Offices	Wimpey
Velvet House	Granby Row	44	Formerly a section of Bombay Street	Wimpey Homes
Chetham's	Victoria Street / Walkers Croft	220	Educational Institution (part of Chetham's)	Chetham's
Smithfield Estate		116	Site of former market	Manchester City Council
Piccadilly Village		136	Reclaimed heavy industrial land	Trafford Park Estates
Lambert Hall	Granby Row	167	Cleared Site	UMIST
4	Fairfield Street	32	Warehouse	Maple Grove
Weston Building	Sackville Street	450	Car Park	UMIST
Orient House	Granby Row	171	Educational Building	Housing Projects Ltd
Castle Quay	Chester Road	38	Warehouses	Manchester Ship Canal Company
Total		2,182		

Source: Manchester City Council

There was a noticeable trend emerging in Manchester. While many of the properties were for sale on the open market, a significant portion were 'affordable' and in many cases, as shown in the table above, operated by housing associations such Tung Sing Housing and Northern Counties. Location-wise, many of the residential developments were located next to or near water (be it a river or canal). As a sign of investor (and city council) confidence, some of them were in gateway locations and, thereby, became 'landmark' developments (a good example being 'Castle Quay' on Chester Road by Manchester Ship Canal Company, a £25 million project which was completed in 1992).

The second trend was the growth of warehouse conversions. Developers Urban Splash secured significant coverage with the conversion of the Smithfield Buildings in the Northern Quarter, completed in 1998. As city-centre and loft living became a hot product, the company focused on opportunities elsewhere. The conversion of six Victorian mill buildings, known as Britannia Mills, was Urban Splash's first-ever scheme in Castlefield. The building was a former mill which had been derelict for seven years by the time they acquired the site in 1997. Construction commenced in March 1998, and the scheme was completed in June 2000, delivering 125 apartments.

▶   Castle Quay, Chester Road.

© Euan Kellie

© Euan Kellie

▲   Britannia Mills.

Further Urban Splash conversions took place in Castlefield, including the former Smerfit Factory on Worseley Street, a 1920s Art Deco warehouse, which was converted to 'The Box Works'. It was the first scheme in Manchester where shell spaces were sold to purchasers who wanted to work with their own architect and design their own home. Construction commenced in February 2001 and was complete in June 2002.

Suddenly the derelict remains of Manchester's glorious industrial past were proving to be an asset that everyone wanted. The city-centre population was swelling. On 31 July 1999 *The Independent* summed the situation up perfectly with their headline:

'Property: It's grand up North'

In the same article the paper estimated that the city-centre population had swelled to 5,000 – a fivefold increase in 10 years.

Anthony H. Wilson, a.k.a. 'Mr Manchester', could also see what was happening. *The Guardian* on 5 January 2001 published his thoughts:

'Manchester is poised. Something is coming. It feels very exciting. Let's see what happens with all these buildings, all these lofts. There is going to be a real explosion in 2003 and 2004 when the centre of Manchester is really lived in like no other city.'

As, one by one, vacant buildings were converted, developers began to look elsewhere and consider other options. Suddenly they began out-bidding each other for sites that, in the past, had been secured for office development. According to an article published by journal *Business Design* on 12 May 2000, Nicholson Estates bought two adjoining office buildings previously owned by Royal & Sun Alliance on St Mary's Parsonage near to the River Irwell. The first £1 million apartment was sold within weeks of unveiling the 20-unit scheme known as Century Buildings. This, along with other projects, led to the disappearance of more than 500,000sq ft (46,450m^2) of office space from the market as residential developers scoured the city for sites.

▼ Century Buildings, Parsonage Gardens.

REBUILDING **MANCHESTER**

► Box Works.

▼ Timber Wharf.

The city-centre formula was working. In addition to the conversions, new buildings began to appear on the skyline. Urban Splash identified the Timber Wharf site in Castlefield as the most appropriate location for their first new-build project (located adjacent to The Box Works). High-quality design was a prerequisite. Accordingly, an architectural competition was held in 2001. The brief made it clear that innovative contemporary design was sought, with creative solutions to the internal layout. Glen Howells Architects were duly selected from over 100 entrants.

The scheme, completed in 2002, went on to pick up a host of awards, including RIBA Housing Design Award 2003, National Home Builder Design Award 2005 for 'Best Brownfield Development' and the Civic Trust Award 2004.

▲ Hacienda, 1999.

One scheme that attracted great attention and interest was that of the Hacienda development, led by Crosby Homes and designed by Stephenson Bell. The nightclub, a warehouse at 11–13 Whitworth Street West on the south side of the Rochdale Canal, opened in 1982 and operated until 1997 when it was closed for the final time.

▼ Hacienda, Whitworth Street West.

Crosby Homes, who acquired the site, held a charity auction on Saturday 25 November 2000 where attendees could acquire memorabilia from the club, including emergency exit lights and the DJ booth box. The scheme caused consternation among key members of Manchester's heritage, including a veteran of the club and author of the definitive history of 'Madchester' music, Dave Haslam. In an article published by *The Guardian* on 29 August 2002 he outlined his dismay:

'However controversial it was, the Hacienda was a cultural asset to Manchester. It helped bring that sense of civic pride back to Manchester. A block of flats built by Crosby Homes is never going to do that.'

The building was demolished in 2002 and replaced with 130 apartments.

▲ Hacienda demolition.

© Aidan O'Rourke - www.aidan.co.uk

▲ Hacienda apartments.

▼ Deansgate Quay site before redevelopment, 1998.

Another scheme of note, also promoted by Crosby Homes, was Deansgate Quay, designed by Stephenson Bell. The proposed buildings were located to the rear of Atlas Bar off Deansgate and included four blocks varying in height from five to seven storeys. Again, the boundary of the city centre was beginning to expand, with former industrial land being re-used piece by piece.

The project went on in 2001 to win a Housing Design Award in recognition of the design excellence.

◀ Deansgate
Quay.

Stephenson Bell

REBUILDING **MANCHESTER**

▶ Piccadilly Village.

Tony Watt

▼ Slate Wharf.

ADC Architects Limited

LARGE-SCALE NEW APARTMENT BUILDINGS

A further addition to the residential market was that of large residential developments comprising a mixture of uses. This trend that began to arrive in the mid-to-late 1990s had, in truth, already begun in Manchester in the late 1980s by way of two schemes that were way ahead of their time. The delivery of these schemes has again played a role in increasing the city-centre population and helping to expand the city-centre boundary.

The first was Piccadilly Village, designed by architects Halliday Meecham. The scheme, located at Millbank Street and Chapeltown Street, came about via a CDMC grant to developers Moran Holdings and Trafford Park Estates to build 125 homes between Piccadilly Station and Great Ancoats Street, on either side of the Ashton Canal. The scheme, which cost £10.5 million provided 125 new houses and flats, 15 craft studios, six shops and 16,000sq ft (1,500m^2) of office space. The project was constructed between 1990 and 1994.

The second was Slate Wharf, which was located at the other end of the CMDC boundary in Castlefield. This development comprised 96 one and two-bedroom canalside apartments in two private courtyards with the luxury of a reclaimed canal basin. ADC Architects were responsible for the scheme that was delivered by Macbryde Homes Ltd between 1994 and 1996. According to Mike Macpherson of ADC Architects, design was a key issue back in 1993:

'In 1993 the CMDC (as planning authority) were insistent on restricting the scale of the proposed Slate Wharf development so that it was similar to that of the surrounding warehouses, both in form, scale and materials, so as to be in keeping with its location within the Castlefield conservation area and Britain's first Urban Heritage Park.'

Following the completion of the Slate Wharf development, Macbryde Homes went on to build a second phase of the development (Jackson's Wharf) which had 47 one, two and three-bedroom flats in a private courtyard off Blantyre Street, also in Castlefield.

▲ Manchester Green Quarter from CIS Tower, 2005.

During the first decade of the new millennium several major new-build schemes have emerged in Manchester city centre. By the beginning of 2010 some were complete, while others had stalled. What is noticeable is that they are all located on the city-centre boundary – a clear demonstration of the city council's desire to extend the city centre.

GREEN QUARTER

The derelict site, which had historically been occupied by mills and worker accommodation, was acquired in 1999 by Crosby Homes with an existing planning consent for 413 units. Their vision was to create a new quarter for the city. A masterplan for the scheme was subsequently prepared and approved by Manchester City Council in June 2004. Following various revisions to the masterplan, the scheme has delivered over 1,300 residential units, open space, a hotel and office space.

▼ Green Quarter prior to development, November 1998.

▲ Macintosh Mills, Cambridge Street..

MACINTOSH VILLAGE

The proposal, designed initially by Sir Terry Farrell and presented to Manchester City Council in 2001, was a £130 million 'flagship redevelopment' which included the listed Macintosh Mills and the construction of a number of new buildings, including a pair of tall buildings situated on either side of Cambridge Street. In overall terms, the Macintosh Mill proposals sought to provide approximately 500 apartments, penthouses and live/work units, along with 21,527sq ft (2,000m²) of commercial space.

Delivery on site has not been quite as prompt as planned. The landmark 11-storey Green Building, designed by Terry Farrell & Partners, which includes 32 flats, a medical clinic and a private day-care institution for 120 children, was completed in 2005 as the first on the site, functioning today as a landmark for the new neighbourhood.

◄ Green Building, designed by Sir Terry Farrell.

SMITHFIELD

The former Smithfield Market, located at the northern end of Shudehill and within the Northern Quarter, was an area of opportunity. To deliver a successful scheme that would also advance the regeneration of this part of the city, a partnership model was put to use in the late 1990s. Muse Developments entered into a joint venture development with Crosby Homes (known as Ician Developments) and Manchester City Council who were the landowners.

A masterplan was prepared, and during the 'noughties' four phases were delivered. The first phase comprised the refurbishment of the former historic fish market walls and the regeneration of a listed building to create a large public courtyard framed by a combination of new and old buildings.

▲ Smithfield Market.

▼ Aerial image of the former Smithfield Market, prior to redevelopment.

REBUILDING **MANCHESTER**

▶ Smithfield – Phase 1.

Ician Developments

▲ Smithfield – Phase 2 (Design House).

▼ Smithfield – Phase 3 (Icon 25).

Ician Developments

Ician Developments

▼ Aerial image of Smithfield.

Ician Developments

Ician Developments

◄ Smithfield – Phase 4 (Crowne Plaza).

The second phase was completed in 2004 and comprised a mix of retail units and space for financial and professional services. Phase three followed in 2006, with 300,000sq ft (185,800m²) of both residential and commercial space. In 2008 phase four was completed, the Crowne Plaza hotel, located on Shudehill designed by architects Mark Weintruab.

Further phases are in the pipeline, including another hotel, further commercial elements and a new central public square – Smithfield Square.

POTATO WHARF

Developers Crosby Lend Lease secured planning permission in 2006 and 2007 that would allow them to build 230 apartments on the north and south sides of Potato Wharf, within the Castlefield conservation area. The apartments would be accommodated in five plots:

Plot 1: Two new buildings, each six storeys in height (Block 1 and 2).

Plot 2: A surface-level car park.

Plot 3: A terrace of 10 three-storey townhouses.

Plot 4: A 13-storey building (Block 3).

Plot 5: A single-storey substation.

▼ Visualisation of Potato Wharf.

Chris Bamford / Virtual Planit

▲ City Gate apartments.

CITY GATE

The expansion of the city centre continued with Bellway Homes introducing the City Gate development, located off Chester Road, designed by Calderpeel architects. The scheme includes three separate residential towers, one at 14 storeys and two at 7 storeys. The various elements were delivered in three phases between 2003 and 2007, known as City Gate, City Gate 2 and City Gate 3.

© Euan Kellie

▲▼ Leftbank.

LEFTBANK

Located within Spinningfields on the banks of the River Irwell, Leftbank has been developed by Westbury Homes (now part of Persimmon Homes), providing approximately 400 apartments. The scheme is also home to restaurants such as Café Rouge, Strada, Ha Ha, Zizzi and Gourmet Burger Kitchen.

By February 2003, according to city council statistics, Manchester had the fastest-growing city centre in Britain. The data was fascinating. By this time there were:

- 62 converted schemes (3,035 units).
- 50 new-build schemes (4,301 units).
- Nine schemes containing a mixture of the two types (1,215 units).

© Euan Kellie

▼ Construction of No.1 Deansgate.

© Aidan O'Rourke - www.aidan.co.uk

© Aidan O'Rourke - www.aidan.co.uk

© Aidan O'Rourke - www.aidan.co.uk

TALL BUILDINGS

As city-centre living in Manchester became hot property, land became scarce. Developers began to look at ways in which to maximise value (and the number of apartments) from sites. Forming part of Edaw's masterplan for the bomb-damaged area and located in the retail core, the 60m-high building, branded as **No.1 Deansgate** and designed by Ian Simpson Architects, was completed in October 2002.

The project formed part of the Shambles West development and consists of 17 storeys of 84 apartments, including eight penthouses. By the time of completion the building was both the UK's tallest all-steel residential building and the first building in Manchester to house a £2 million property (the honour of which went to the duplex penthouses on the 16th and 17th floors). The building, designed by Ian Simpson Architects, was described by the RIBA as the 'heroic symbol of the regeneration of the city centre of Manchester' and went on to win a plethora of awards (including Roses Design Awards, Best Residential Project 2002; National Built in Quality Awards 2003; RIBA Design Housing Award 2003; Civic Trust Award 2004).

▼ No.1 Deansgate.

© Aidan O'Rourke - www.aidan.co.uk

▲ Construction of No.1 Deansgate.

▲ Completion of No.1 Deansgate.

REBUILDING **MANCHESTER**

© Aidan O'Rourke - www.aidan.co.uk

The promotional literature for No. 1 Deansgate from developers Crosby Homes, outlined in the book *The Anxious City: British Urbanism in the Late 20th century*, was certainly compelling:

'Put your feet up. Far off are empty hills, above you the sky. But beneath is the bustling, ant-like activity of Manchester's prime corporate, commercial and leisure district. You are all-seeing but totally uninvolved. And the feeling this brings – of deep relaxation; of unwinding – is almost palpable.'

As indicated in the 'Commercial' chapter, prime sites in the city centre with planning permissions in place for office developments were trading for high prices as developers sought to provide residential opportunities. This was typified by the piece of vacant land sandwiched in between the Free Trade Hall and Great Northern Warehouse. Designed by Assael Architects and promoted by George Wimpey, the project known as the **Great Northern Tower** secured planning permission on 2002 for a scheme rising up to 25 storeys, clad in glass, metal and grey tiles. The *Manchester Evening News*, in an article published on 21 July 2004, recognised what was happening:

'Two years ago George Wimpey City paid £8m for the prime quarter-acre Great Northern Tower site – a deal which put residential land in Manchester in the same price league as London, New York and Tokyo.'

◀ Great Northern Tower.

The trend continued with the **Beetham Tower**. The site, located at the junction of Great Bridgewater Street, Liverpool Road and Deansgate, had for many years been identified by the city council as a 'gateway' location suitable for a landmark building. The 1967 City Centre Map published images showing a scale model of the city centre, and remarkably two of these images showed a tall building, with podium, on what would become the Beetham site! The vision at the time was to introduce a comprehensive development area for the 'Central Station area' ahead of the closure of Central Station (which took place in 1969).

Moving into the 1990s and the site, which originally formed Phase 3 of the Great Northern Warehouse redevelopment proposals, was sold to Hilton Hotel in 1999 who went on to secure planning permission for an eight-storey hotel comprising 349 bedrooms. By 2002, however, the scheme had not been built due to the absence of the necessary sufficient critical mass of people and commercial activity to sustain a Hilton hotel on what was the edge of the commercial core. The undeveloped site comprised two pieces: American car showroom, Bauer Millett, was located in the final piece of the former railway viaduct, while land to the rear was in use as a surface car park.

As a consequence, in 2002 Hilton approached a number of developers and held a selected developer and architectural competition in order to generate options for the site. Hilton wanted the winning scheme to be commercially deliverable and of very high quality, incorporating a Hilton Hotel on the site. The Beetham Organisation proposals, which included a scheme designed by Ian Simpson Architects, were the successful entry on the basis of quality and deliverability and they entered into a development agreement with Hilton.

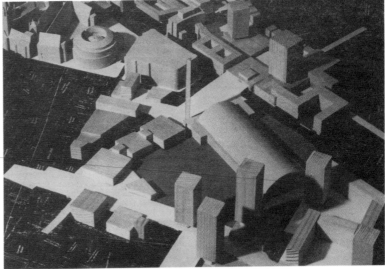

▲ Tall buildings on the Beetham site – taken from the 1967 city-centre map.

Manchester City Council

▼ Beetham Tower site before development.

© Aidan O'Rourke - www.aidan.co.uk

© Euan Kellie

▲ Clearance of the Beetham site, March 2004.

© Aidan O'Rourke - www.aidan.co.uk

▲ Beetham Tower under construction.

▼ Beetham Tower under construction.

© Aidan O'Rourke - www.aidan.co.uk

Following detailed discussions with Manchester City Council as well as English Heritage and CABE, the Government's advisory body in respect of architecture and the built environment, two planning applications were submitted to Manchester City Council in June 2003. The first sought consent to demolish the remaining piece of the railway viaduct (this was necessary as it was listed), the other for a scheme that would be built in two phases: a 48-storey building (Phase 1) with 219 residential apartments, a 285-bed Hilton Hotel, notably with a bar on the 23rd floor, and a 70,000sq ft (6,500m²) office building (Phase 2).

Both applications were approved unanimously by Manchester City Council Planning Committee on 23 October 2003, and the celebrations began. The decision received national attention, with *The Independent* leading on 28 October 2003 with the headline:

'Tall storeys: Mancunians head for Britain's highest living rooms.'

In the same article architect Ian Simpson expressed his delight:

'This is an amazing project for our practice and for Manchester. I believe we have created what could be a spectacular addition to the Manchester skyline.'

The final approved tall building was 157m (520ft) high, with 48 storeys. It was claimed that on a clear day it might be possible, from the top of the tower, to be able to see as far as Snowdonia, Blackpool and Liverpool. Construction commenced in early 2004, and by the time the building was 'topped out' on 26 April 2006 all apartments had been sold. Rumours of celebrities acquiring apartments in the tower came thick and fast. According to the website beethamtower.org, the building was home to Shayne Ward (winner of the second series of *X-Factor*) and footballers Phil and Gary Neville, along with Cristiano Ronaldo. The only piece which by 2010 had not been delivered was that of Phase 2: the adjacent office building.

The scheme has won a series of awards. In 2007, the Beetham Tower was awarded Best Building by the Concrete Society Awards, Best Tall Building by The Council on Tall Buildings and Urban Habitats and Project of the Year in North West Regional Construction Awards. A year later it was awarded Project of the Year and Design and Construction Award in the RICS North West Awards.

According to city council data, city living by mid-2005 could be summarised as follows:

• Estimates suggested that 15,000 people were now living in the centre.
• There were nearly 7,000 new residential units in the property pipeline. 4,143 of these were under construction, and 2,857 had the benefit of planning permission.

© Aidan O'Rourke - www.aidan.co.uk

▲▼◄ Beetham Tower under construction.

REBUILDING **MANCHESTER**

▶ Beetham Tower under construction.

▶ Construction complete.

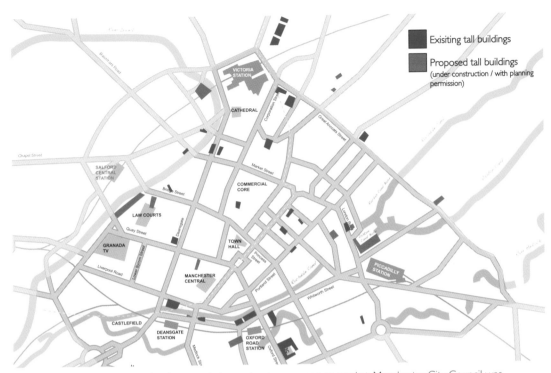

Exisiting tall buildings

Proposed tall buildings
(under construction / with planning permission)

◄ Tall buildings in Manchester city centre (existing and proposed), 2007.

On the back of the Beetham planning permission and a strong property market, Manchester City Council was inundated with applications for residential-led tall building proposals within the city centre and on its fringe. While the council adopted a laissez-faire approach to such proposals, there was a rigorous commitment to high-quality design. Two of the most notable schemes that followed the Beetham model of a residential/hotel development included the Eastgate Tower and Albany Tower.

The **Albany Tower**, designed by Ian Simpson Architects and promoted by Liverpool-based developer Albany Assets, benefitted from a prominent location, located on Aytoun Street and adjacent to the Rochdale Canal, across the road from the Piccadilly Place development. The site was home to a derelict property known as the Crown Building previously occupied by the Labour Exchange, part of the Department of Employment. As the proposals became public knowledge the *Manchester Evening News*, on 23 December 2004, excitedly captured the spirit of the moment, describing the Albany Tower proposals as:

'the latest in a string of proposed skyscrapers set to change the shape of Manchester, turning it into a British answer to Manhattan.'

▼ Vacant Crown Building on Aytoun Street / Auburn Street.

149

REBUILDING **MANCHESTER**

▶ Visualisation of Albany Tower.

▼ Visualisation of Albany Tower from Piccadilly Station.

The scheme which was submitted for planning permission in February 2005, sought consent for a 44-storey building comprising 237 apartments, 11-storey office building with 150,000sq ft (14,000m^2) of space, a restaurant and shop, 200 car parking spaces and public realm which would overlook the canal. The city council offered their full support and outlined the importance of the proposals and the site in the 12 May 2005 Planning Committee Report:

'The current perception is generally that Piccadilly Station is not part of the active core of the City Centre...the application site can [therefore] be seen to hold a crucial and pivotal location in terms of establishing a viable new link between the station [Piccadilly] and important areas within the city centre, helping to integrate the Piccadilly area with the commercial core and substantially improve the quality of this important gateway route from the station into the heat of the city centre.'

Planning permission was subsequently granted by the city council in November 2005. By 2010 construction had still not commenced, however, and the site was still occupied by the vacant and derelict Crown Building.

Another skyscraper that ran in tandem with the Albany Tower was that of the **Eastgate Tower**. Designed by Australian architects Woods Bagot and promoted by developers Inacity, the scheme, located behind Piccadilly Station on a 3.5-acre site between Ducie Street and Store Street, included a 60-storey tower with number of smaller buildings of between eight and 20 storeys. In total, the scheme included 701 flats covering 604,000sq ft (56,000m²), a 220 bedroom hotel, a 25,000sq ft (2,300m²) fitness centre, an 18,000sq ft (1,600m²) conference facility, and bars and restaurants.

These were grand plans. At 617ft, the building would have been 26ft taller than Swiss Re's 30 St Mary Axe (commonly known as 'The Gherkin') in the City of London. The scheme was approved by the city council on 17 March 2005. Sadly, like the Albany Tower proposals, by 2010 the scheme had not been built. While the site had been cleared, it was in use only as a temporary car park.

© Euan Kellie

▲ Eastgate Tower site.

Chris Bamford / Virtual Planit

◄ Visualisation of Eastgate Tower.

REBUILDING **MANCHESTER**

◄▲ Visualisation of Eastgate Tower.

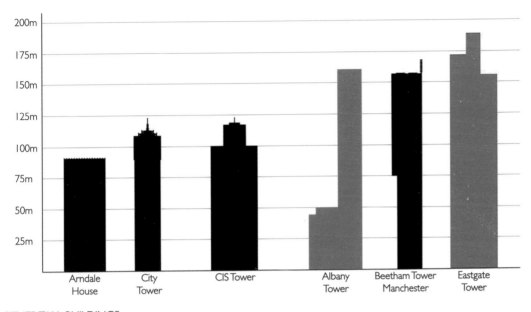

◀ Heights of proposed tall buildings compared to existing.

▲▼ Skyline Central, Rochdale Road.

OTHER TALL BUILDINGS

In the mid-to-late 'noughties' the city continued to attract and support residential-led proposals of real architectural merit. A number of these were delivered.

Skyline Central on Rochdale Road, by developers West Properties and designed by architects Jacobs Webber, was granted planning permission in 2004 and constructed between 2005 and 2006. The building secured the Built in Quality Award in 2007. Another wonderful contribution to Manchester's city-centre fringe has been that of the 21-storey Islington Wharf, designed by Broadway Malyan architects. Comprising 200 residential units, the scheme took 18 months to build and was complete in early 2009.

35-storey Gravity Tower on Store Street, designed by Austin-Smith:Lord; and Vivo at Owen Street, also designed by Ian Simpson Architects which included five buildings, ranging in height from 14 to 49 storeys. Undoubtedly, the global economic meltdown and the long, deep and dark UK recession played its role.

Other innovative residential-led tall-building developments that had been granted planning permission but which, sadly, by 2010 had not progressed included the 28-storey Project Sharp, located on Sharp Street and Rochdale Road, designed by Ian Simpson Architects for West Properties. It seems almost fitting that this chapter should end by presenting what may be,

◀ Visualisation of Gravity Tower.

© Aidan O'Rourke - www.aidan.co.uk

153

REBUILDING **MANCHESTER**

▼▲▶   Islington Wharf, designed by architects Broadway Malyan.

The Challenge of a Living City

As more and more residential developments were delivered in the city centre and people moved in, communities were forged – such as those in Castlefield, The Village and the Northern Quarter. Land became more and more scarce, values increased and, consequently, the bond of trust between the city council and all players in the development process was pushed to the limit. In the latter half of the noughties, two case studies captured these challenges beautifully. By 2010 one had succeeded in terms of securing planning permission, while the other had not.

Approved

In October 2005 developers West Properties acquired a site located at the junction of Whitworth Street and Princess Street, in the heart of Manchester's Gay Village. At the time it was a low-quality surface car park (only 0.51 hectares in size), but it was a site of value to many. It was also located in the Whitworth Street/Princess Street conservation area and was surrounded by Victorian warehouse buildings that had been converted to residential apartments, including the listed Regency House, Amazon House, 3 Brazil Street and 42–44 Sackville Street.

The site had been vacant for almost 15 years following the demolition of the last of four warehouse buildings in 1993. The four buildings that previously occupied the site were known as Number 1 and 2 Brazil Street, Number 113 Princess Street, Whitworth Street House and Somerset House. As a first step, West Properties appointed Ian Simpson Architects (following a design competition) to commence initial design studies to assess the options for the site.

▲ The Origin site, Whitworth Street.

◄ Visualisation of 'Origin', Princess Street.

Courtesy of West Properties

To deliver the scheme consultation with a host of key parties would be an absolute priority. This included residents, community groups, businesses, city council officers, and English Heritage. The process began in December 2005. Design and height were ultimately going to be two key issues for discussion. An early version of the scheme was presented during initial stages of public consultation; it was then amended and presented to CABE and English Heritage in July 2006, again as part of the early pre-submission discussions. As part of this vision the residential element, which fronted onto Whitworth Street, was 24 storeys in height. This concerned English Heritage, who asked for a redesign. Discussions continued, and by the time the scheme (now known as 'Origin') was eventually submitted for planning permission in October 2006 there were four key elements: a central landscaped public open space, 13-storey hotel, 7-storey office block with 87,039sq ft (8,086m^2) and a 16-storey residential building with 180 units.

Like the Free Trade Hall (see 'Historic' chapter), this was an application that generated significant levels of interest. According to the city council Planning Committee report, dated 18 January 2007, 239 letters of objection were submitted (as well as 64 in support) along with a petition with 413 signatures. A website was also set up so residents could easily view all the planning application documents and be kept informed of progress. A major area of contention was the style of architecture and the height, particularly within a conservation area and in close proximity to so many listed buildings. Some of the comments submitted to the city council during the planning process included:

'The proposed design is seriously out of scale with the surrounding buildings. The area is known as "The Village", and any new design should address this fact, suggesting as it does buildings of modest size and proportions.'

'I would see nothing but a mass of glass out of my window, I would not only lack light, but I would not see any sky at all.'

'Local residents would not only be in total darkness, we would also suffer loss of open space, loss of trees, and no public space as the area in between buildings would be nothing more than a wind tunnel, as has happened with other developments.'

'PLEASE, PLEASE, PLEASE do not allow this development to go ahead.'

In a letter dated 14 November 2006 sent to Chris Speck of the Whitworth Street Conservation Area Residents Group, and copied to Sir Howard Bernstein, English Heritage outlined their position:

'Whilst we would still prefer a scheme of both lower density and height we accept that the current heights and massing, especially the reduction in height to Whitworth Street, are an acceptable compromise and therefore withdraw our previous objections in principle.'

▼   Community Petros / Princess Street
     development website.

Welcome to the community Petros/Princess Street development website.

On 14th November 2006 a formal planning permission application to Manchester City Council was accepted from West Properties to develop the Petros Car Park Site that neighbours Regency House, Whitworth Street, Central Manchester. The application was officially submitted 1st November 2006, and the official reference number is 081209. A second planning application (Ref 081371) has also been made to demolish the existing historic walls around this site.

For a structured summary of all the application details please click here.

A prominent public campaign against the development is in progress. We believe the new development will change the appearance of the conservation area where we all live, work and socialise in a negative way. The style, height and mass of the buildings is inappropriate for this small site and inconsiderate of the historic surroundings. Click here for the latest campaign updates on the SAVE OUR VILLAGE blog.

Latest: The planning committee visited the site on 15th February 2007 and requested some further amendments to the scheme. This was well covered by BBC Look NorthWest, click here to view. The amendments agreed are only a 3m reduction in height at the Whitworth Street junction of Venice Street.

The official council site with the main planning application is here. The official council site for the secondary planning application is here. The official West Properties site about the development is available here. This had recently had problems, so I have a mirror of this site here.

Page last updated 24/3/2007. Also check the Save Our Village Campaign Blog. Please check back regularly as this site is updated.

Contact Me

www.petros.ourflat.co.uk

◄ 'Origin' site hoardings, April 2010.

This was a position shared by CABE. In a letter to the city council dated 24 November 2006 they outlined their support for the scheme:

'...which seems to us to provide high-quality architecture, a clear relationship to the street and site, and welcome the provision of public space within a mixed use complex. We think the design is an improvement on earlier iterations and we would be happy to see it built.'

For the city council it was a question of balance. Following further slight amendments to the height of the residential block, the scheme was approved in March 2007 following two appearances at the city council's Planning Committee (BBC North West also appeared at the second Planning Committee, such was the level of interest). In September 2008 further alterations were made to the hotel building and associated public realm to accommodate the specific operational requirements of W Hotel (part of the Starwood Group) – specifically, an increase of 12.7m. Approval was again granted in October 2008. It is important to reflect and consider this position against other projects that encountered turbulence. Trust, ownership and consultation had led to a scheme deemed by the city council to be appropriate, in a highly sensitive location. By 2010 work had started at the site but paused as the global economic crisis took hold.

REBUILDING **MANCHESTER**

▶ Vacant Jackson's Wharf pub, Castlefield, February 2009.

Refused

A planning application in Manchester city centre does not, however, guarantee a planning permission. In May 2007 proposals were put forward by developers Peel Holdings, designed by Ian Simpson Architects, to redevelop the site occupied by the vacant Jackson's Wharf pub in Castlefield and deliver an apartment building seven storeys in height with 118 flats and a retail unit on the ground floor. In terms of design it was 'L' shaped in plan, with the two long edges of the 'L' set along Blantyre Street and along the western boundary of the site.

The scheme, like the 'Origin' proposals, was in a conservation area, this time Castlefield. The planning application generated significant levels of opposition, with over 100 individual objections. According to the Pride of Manchester website, those opposed to the scheme included Take That's Jason Orange and Olympic swimmer James Hickman. Broadcaster Mike Harding made public his vehement opposition to the project, published on the Pride of Manchester website:

'The original concept of Castlefield as an urban heritage park and the early work of Jim Ramsbottom in particular was truly exciting. Then the big money moved in and the dream was hijacked. Brutal Euroboxes, with neither imagination nor taste to ameliorate them, were thrown up in piecemeal in one of the worst cases of planning blight I can think of, so that now Manchester looks like a city designed by a schizophrenic drunk with attention deficiency disorder.'

Despite amendments to the design following concerns raised by city council members at a Planning Committee in December 2007, and no objection from English Heritage, the scheme was refused against officer's recommendation of approval on 17 January 2008. Peel Holdings appealed against the decision and a public inquiry was held in November 2008. The Planning Inspectorate, again, chose to refuse the proposal. Particular attention and weight was given to the Castlefield conservation area and its defining features – identified in the Planning Inspector's report as the 'solid and powerful construction of the warehouses.'

▼ Pride of Manchester website – opposing the Jackson's Wharf proposals.

© Euan Kellie

◄ Left to right: Premier House and the Renaissance Hotel, April 2010.

as of 2010, one of the final tall building proposals in Manchester city centre for some time. In a further twist, it involves a site that is the only remaining area within the bomb masterplan that had not been redeveloped.

The scheme, designed by Ian Simpson Architects and put forward by developers West Properties, proposed the demolition of the Renaissance Hotel, along with the office building Premier House. The site would be cleared and replaced with four buildings which would vary in height from 10 storeys to 35 storeys and would deliver 248 residential units.

The site was previously known as Shambles West and formed part of the Market Place development delivered in the early 1970s. The scheme faced Shambles East and was connected across Deansgate by a pedestrian footbridge which was demolished in 1999. The 15-storey tower, which subsequently became the Ramada Hotel, was designed as offices by architects Cruickshank and Seward in 1972.

The proposals were supported and approved by Manchester City Council in June 2009. In the Planning Committee report published in January 2009, CABE outlined their support:

'CABE admires the intelligence of this scheme and the skill with which the design team has responded to the brief and the challenges presented by the site...overall it is felt the benefits this scheme will bring to the city of Manchester will ensure it is regarded as a fitting final piece of redevelopment in line with the post-bombing masterplan for the City Centre.'

▼ Visualisation of Premier House.

Courtesy of West Properties

REBUILDING **MANCHESTER**

▶ Residential schemes in Manchester city centre, 2010.

CONCLUSION

The rejuvenation of Manchester's city-centre population is to be admired. The increase from 900 residents in 1991 to 19,000 in 2009 is truly remarkable. It has also led to some fine examples of architecture across, and now outside, the city centre. The Beetham Tower, a product of this trend, has also made the most noticeable change to the city's skyline. Not everyone likes the building but, to a certain extent, that is not the point. What is important is that it is distinctive and is something that people can associate with Manchester..

While encouraging city-centre residential development has been a good thing, there has been another side to the story. As land has become scarce and the population has grown, the city council has, on many occasions, had to adopt a balanced approach to decision making when confronted by sensitive issues such as the perceived impact of a proposed development on the amenity of existing residents. This has been captured perfectly by the 'Origin' and Jackson's Wharf proposals.

The challenge for the future will be maintaining and increasing the population while introducing families and associated community facilities, most likely to take place on the fringe of the city centre. This is characterised by some of the exciting, emerging projects such as New Islington and Ancoats Urban Village.

'[Manchester] does not have an icon like the Eiffel Tower, the Sydney Harbour Bridge, or the Empire State Building which immediately denotes the city of origin. Its icon is the cityscape of new and older buildings.'

– Peter Saville

HISTORIC

BEFORE THE BOMB

One of the greatest challenges when seeking to deliver a truly international city centre is finding the balance between the delivery of new development and investment and preserving and enhancing sensitive buildings and areas that form a major part of the city's unique character. Manchester city centre has been no different. This is captured wonderfully by graphic designer Peter Saville, famed for his Factory Records front covers – in the quote at the top of this page.

The presence of such a cityscape, supported by grand pieces of architecture delivered during the halcyon days of the late 19th and early 20th century (and in some cases even earlier) has made it a veritable 'hot potato' subject for some. The story begins with the 1945 City of Manchester plan, which was fiercely critical of the city centre's existing architecture:

'The city's buildings, with few exceptions, are undistinguished. Moreover, our few noteworthy buildings are obscured by the dense development surrounding them.'

Rather than retain, restore and cherish many of the buildings that typified Manchester's golden industrial age, the plan outlined their wholesale replacement with 'huge, identical pavilion buildings'. Literally, almost all of them. Aside from the Cathedral, which was to be restored and set in formal gardens linking it with Chetham's School of Music, other notable structures were to be sacrificed for other development. Incredibly, this included the 'civic group' in the city centre, which comprised the Town Hall, Town Hall extension and Central Library, fronting on to Albert Square:

'Whatever the architectural merits of these buildings may be – and the attempt to reconcile the Gothic revivalism of Waterhouse's original Town Hall with a more modern style in the recently added extension cannot be regarded as entirely successful – the general impression is one of congestion.'

REBUILDING **MANCHESTER**

Heritage Glossary

Listed Building

A listed building is a building (or structure) that has been designated as being of 'special architectural or historic interest'. Listed buildings are graded I, II* and II. Grade I and II* are particularly important buildings of outstanding interest. Together they amount to eight per cent of all listed buildings. The remaining 92 per cent are of special interest and are listed Grade II.

Conservation Area

The special character of these areas does not come from the quality of their buildings alone. It can also relate to the historic layout of roads, paths and boundaries; characteristic building and paving materials; a particular 'mix' of building uses; public and private spaces, such as gardens, parks and greens; and trees and street furniture, which contribute to particular views – all these and more make up the familiar local scene. Conservation areas give broader protection than listing individual buildings: all the features, listed or otherwise, within the area, are recognised as part of its character.

Scheduled Ancient Monument

Scheduled monuments are nationally important archaeological sites designated and added to a schedule by the Government on the advice provided by English Heritage. Generally, scheduled monuments do not include buildings in use.

The absence of what would become known as 'civic awareness' (across the UK, a trend not exclusive to Manchester) was something that began to appear on the Government's radar shortly after World War Two.

The 'listing' of historic buildings started in 1950 as part of a growing awareness of the need to preserve the historic architecture of Britain in the face of post-war building and demolition (rather than re-use) of buildings. Some of the first designations in Manchester city centre which appeared in 1952 are outlined below:

Building	Grade	Date
Rylands Library.	I	25 January 1952
Nos.25 to 31 (odd), and former chapel at rear of No.31.	II	25 February 1952
Town Hall.	I	25 February 1952
Cathedral Church of St Mary.	I	25 January 1952
Former Bank of England, King Street.	I	25 February 1952
Nos.35 and 37 with attached railings, King Street.	II	25 February 1952
Nos.38 and 42, Royal Bank of Scotland, Mosley Street (formerly listed as No.38).	II*	25 February 1952
City Art Gallery, Mosley Street.	I	25 February 1952
No.57, Portico Library.	II*	25 February 1952
Britannia Hotel, Portland Street.	II*	25 February 1952
Church of St Ann, St Ann's Street.	I	25 February 1952
Nos.8 and 8a, 10, 12 to 16, 18 and 20, 22, St John Street (north side).	II	25 February 1952
Nos.11 to 17, 19, 21 to 25, St John Street (south side).	II	25 February 1952
Sinclair's Oyster Bar, Shambles Square.	II	25 February 1952
The Old Wellington Inn.	II	25 February 1952

The Ministry of Housing and Local Government (a government department at the time – previously known as Ministry of Local Government and Planning) went further and prepared what would become an influential report in 1967, entitled 'Preservation and Change'. As the title suggests, the document took account of the high and accelerating rate of urban development across the country and the fact that many buildings of 'grace and distinction' had been lost. To counter the trend, the report suggested that conservation policies be developed for sensitive areas. These would be known as conservation areas.

The outcome was the Civic Amenities Act, introduced by central government at the national level in 1967. Suddenly, across the country the preservation and conservation of old buildings began to take effect. The Town & Country Planning Act 1968 followed shortly after and made it illegal to demolish a listed building without consent, although other buildings in conservation areas were not protected until six years later.

Such legislative changes at the national level filtered down and were reflected in Manchester city centre. Between July 1970 and August 1974, seven conservation areas were designated in the city centre. These allocations brought with them an extra layer of protection for buildings and spaces and demonstrated awareness by the council that there was a need for control.

- St Ann's Square (July 1970).
- St John Street (November 1970).
- Upper King Street (November 1970).
- Albert Square (March 1972).
- Cathedral Area (April 1972).
- St Peter's Square (November 1973).
- Whitworth Street (August 1974).

What happens if historic buildings are demolished without planning permission?

Conservation areas and listed buildings are potentially powerful tools. Should someone choose to demolish a listed building without planning permission then they could face trial in a magistrates court and could potentially enjoy six months in prison and/or a fine up to £20,000. Should the matter reach the crown court, the penalty can be raised to two years prison and/or unlimited fine.

Unauthorised demolition of a whole building or structure in a conservation area is a criminal offence. Other works of development that have been carried out with the necessary planning permission can also be regarded as unauthorised works and the local planning authority can serve an 'enforcement notice' requiring the works to be undone. Should the notice be ignored then the local authority can do the work itself and seek to recover the costs or prosecute.

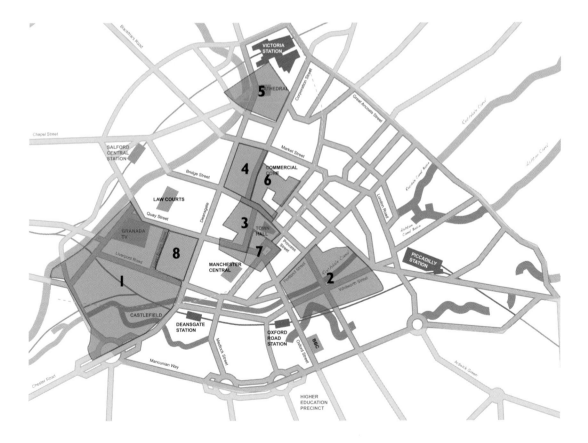

Conservation Areas

1 Castlefield
2 Whitworth Street
3 Albert Square
4 St Ann's Square
5 Cathedral Area
6 Upper King Street
7 St Peter's Square
8 St John Street

◄ City-centre conservation areas, 1984.

▶ The Museum of Science and Industry.

© Aidan O'Rourke - www.aidan.co.uk

In the late 1970s and early 1980s the focus on preservation of buildings in Manchester city centre continued, with some truly innovative solutions. It was time, once again, for Manchester to show others how it should be done. The re-use of buildings, many of which were vacant yet formed an intrinsic part of the city's infrastructure, with a tourist or civic element came about in the late 1970s. In 1978 the Greater Manchester Council agreed to purchase the 1830 part of the vacant Liverpool Road Station from British Rail for the token sum of £1. Five years later, following considerable refurbishment, the North Western Museum of Science and Industry relocated from its temporary premises on Grosvenor Street, Chorlton-on-Medlock and moved into the new building.

Similarly, the re-use of the vacant Royal Exchange was described by Kenneth Powell as the flagship of the conservation movement in the city. This inspired re-use of the building was delivered by way of the Theatre 69 Trust – a public and private partnership. The innovative decision to include a theatre module within the building (designed by architects Levitt Bernstein) was truly dramatic.

▼ Royal Exchange Theatre.

© Euan Kellie

On 13 October 1979 Manchester City Council made the dramatic decision to designate Castlefield a conservation area. This was a radical decision – to most people, even today, a conservation area would typically be associated with buildings of great architectural and civic value. Manchester's former industrial heartland was at the time the complete opposite: derelict and contaminated. Yet the city council believed an opportunity existed to drive regeneration into the area by safeguarding the area's industrial heritage. From Roman remains to Victorian transport infrastructure, Castlefield's wealth of historical interest gave credence to its self-designated title of the UK's first Urban Heritage Park in 1982.

Manchester's creative and dynamic approach to conservation was unusual to say the least, yet highly commendable. This was recognised by CABE:

'...[Manchester City Council's] policy of conserving and adapting its historic buildings and open spaces for tourist and leisure use was unusual at the time compared with action being taken in other areas of urban economic decline.'

In 1983 it published a booklet called *New uses for old buildings* – a showcase of 50 buildings in the city that had been converted between 1973 and 1983. It continued with the transformation of wonderful derelict buildings such as the former railway hub, Central Station, into the Greater Manchester Exhibition Hall (GMEX, now known as Manchester Central). Manchester was, once again, a leader in its field, demonstrating that these landmark buildings were assets rather than liabilities.

▲ GMEX, now known as Manchester Central.

The protection of conservation areas in Manchester city centre continued in the mid-1980s with a series of new designations and the extension of existing areas:

- Albert Square (extended June 1985).
- Ancoats (designated June 1989).
- Parsonage Gardens (designated June 1985).
- Shudehill (designated January 1987).
- Smithfield (designed January 1987).
- George Street (designated June 1985).
- Stevenson Square (designated February 1987, extended December 1987).
- Whitworth Street (extended June 1985).
- Upper King Street (extended June 1985).

The years of the Central Manchester Development Corporation fortified the concept of conservation and protection in Manchester city centre. It immediately inherited an area that contained parts of five conservation areas and 115 listed buildings, two of which were Grade I listed and 11 of which were Grade II*. The corporation took the view that a series of factors had led to the decline of these buildings, such as the high cost of refurbishment, the lack of any clear alternative use for them and the poor quality of the surrounding environment.

Consequently, it was recognised at the outset that these buildings and structures gave Manchester city centre a character that made it interesting,

▼ City-centre conservation areas, 2010.

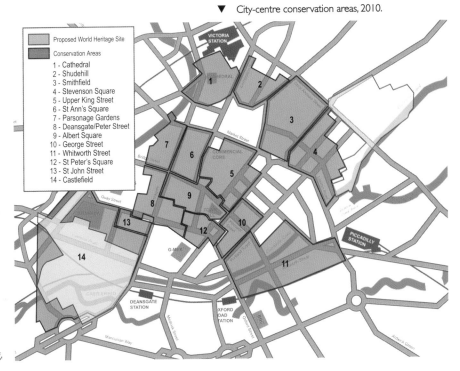

Proposed World Heritage Site
Conservation Areas

1 - Cathedral
2 - Shudehill
3 - Smithfield
4 - Stevenson Square
5 - Upper King Street
6 - St Ann's Square
7 - Parsonage Gardens
8 - Deansgate/Peter Street
9 - Albert Square
10 - George Street
11 - Whitworth Street
12 - St Peter's Square
13 - St John Street
14 - Castlefield

REBUILDING **MANCHESTER**

What is The Planning Inspectorate and a Public Inquiry?

The Planning Inspectorate for England and Wales is an executive agency of the Department for Communities and Local Government of the United Kingdom Government. It is responsible for the determination of planning and enforcement appeals and public examination of local development plans. It also deals with a wide variety of other planning-related casework, including listed building consent appeals, advertisement appeals (about, for instance, shop signs and advertisement displays on hoardings, bus shelters etc), and cases on which inspectors report to the Secretary of State concerned on planning applications requiring ministerial approval.

If a planning application is refused permission the applicant may decide to appeal. It is also possible to ask the Secretary of State to 'call in' a significant planning application, and hold a public inquiry (this is what happened with the Free Trade Hall). These can last for several days, sometimes weeks. Members of the public are allowed to view the spectacle as the witnesses (usually representing the Local Authority and the developer) are cross-examined.

exciting and potentially desirable for future investors. The refurbishment of vacant and under-used buildings and structures of architectural merit become part of the corporation's strategy. There was, however, a balance to be struck, and in delivering 'the greater good' not all areas and buildings could be preserved and retained. This was perhaps reflected by the demolition of the Grade II listed Havelock Mill on 72–78 Great Bridgewater Street in 1995 as part of the office development opposite the Bridgewater Hall.

Notwithstanding, the table below gives a snapshot of the investment and input provided by the CMDC in respect of some of the listed building conversions and how the public-private partnership delivered some important developments.

Scheme	Grade	Use	Cost	CMDC
Castle Quay	2	Residential, retail, offices.	£4.9 million	£1 million
Velvet House	2	Part of Granby Village Housing.	£16.1 million	£3.3 million city grant
Lancaster House	2*	Residential and offices.	£6.8 million	£1.25 million city grant
Orient House	2*	Residential.	£10.2 million	£1.2 million city grant

During the 1990s and leading up to the bomb, Manchester City Council continued to encourage the sensitive enhancement of listed buildings. In November 1994 an RIBA international design competition was launched by the council in respect of the City Art Gallery on Mosley Street. Hopkins Architects were selected as the winners in January 1995. The new extension, with its stone and glass façade, provides a landmark for the city centre, and a spacious new glass atrium was created to link the new wing with the former City Art Gallery and Athenaeum. It was re-opened to the public in May 2002 and went on to secure a host of awards, including the Civic Society of Manchester Phoenix Award 2002, RIBA Award 2003 and the Civic Trust Award 2004.

So, by 11:17am on 15 June 1996 the protection and enhancement of the city centre's heritage was already on the radar.

AFTER THE BOMB

THE BOMB-DAMAGED CORE

The bomb-damaged core presented the task force and Manchester City Council with a fascinating collection of areas and buildings. It comprised six conservation areas Cathedral, Shudehill, Smithfield, Parsonage Gardens, St Ann's Square and Upper King Street, as well as several Grade II and II* listed buildings (two of which were Grade I: the Cathedral and Chetham's Library). There were also two Scheduled Ancient Monuments (Old Wellington and Hanging Ditch on Cateaton Street).

As presented earlier, many of these buildings had been affected superficially, while others had suffered structural damage. Two had been hit particularly hard: The Royal Exchange and the Corn Exchange.

In both cases there were two clear actions: Firstly, detailed investigative work had to be undertaken to ascertain the extent of the damage and to ensure buildings were structurally sound and watertight. Secondly, innovative and sensitive new uses for these buildings had to be delivered in accordance with the broad aims of the masterplan.

As introduced earlier, the Royal Exchange had been badly damaged by the bomb and action was needed urgently. In an interview published by *The Independent* on 16 July 1996, artistic director Braham Murray outlined the position:

'without emergency funding from the Arts Council, we'll close.'

▲　Scaffolding inside the Royal Exchange Theatre.

The planning applications followed. The first was submitted on 23 December 1996 by architects Levitt Bernstein Associates, and the plan was to make alterations to the Exchange Street and Old Bank Street entrances and to make repairs and improvements to the general theatre premises, in light of damage caused by the bomb.

In May 1997 Braham Murray and the rest of the theatre bosses were jubilant when it was announced that £30 million would be made available to refurbish the Exchange. Murray expressed his delight in an interview published by *Manchester Evening News* on 21 May 1997:

'We had planned a refurbishment – now it will be a rebirth'.

▲▼◀　Refurbished Royal Exchange Theatre.

Suddenly the plans were very different. An updated theatre stage would be provided, as well as a second 120-seat theatre. The distinctive glass domes would also be re-glazed in blue glass, while coffee bars would be added to create a link between Cross Street and St Ann's Square. On 5 February 1998 a further application was submitted for reinstatement works following the bomb damage – as with many of the proposals at the time, consent was granted by Manchester City Council in eight weeks.

The works were completed by June 1998, and the theatre re-opened on 30 November 1998. Fittingly, the first show was the *Lancashire Life* play Hindle Wakes, the show that was being staged on the day of the bomb in 1996.

The situation was similar for the Corn Exchange. In the early part of 1997 the proposals for the Corn Exchange were submitted by architects The Ratcliff Partnership on behalf of Frogmore Estates. The initial scheme (Phase 1), which sought to repair the building in

▲▼ Refurbishment of the Corn Exchange.

▼ Corn Exchange dome.

▲ 'The Triangle', opening Autumn 1999, taken in October 1998.

▲ 'The Triangle', 2001.

light of the damage and devastation, was approved by the council in April 1997. A year later Phase 2 was submitted, with the objective of refurbishing the building (internally and externally) and introducing a series of uses such as food, drink, retail and nightclub, along with office space on the upper floors. The objective of prompt determination continued, and consent was granted on 10 September 1998.

In the two years that followed, significant work was undertaken at the Corn Exchange, and it slowly became the retail scheme known as 'The Triangle'. The scheme was completed in 2000 and opened to the public on 22 August 2000. Further information can be found on the project in the 'Retail' chapter.

▼ The Triangle, Exchange Square, 2010.

The 'Shambles' Pubs

The lynchpin to Edaw's masterplan was the delivery of a new pedestrianised street that would connect Manchester Cathedral with St Ann's Square and St Ann's Church. One slight problem was that two historic pubs were in the way: The Old Wellington and Sinclair's Oyster Bar, concealed within the concrete prison of Shambles Square.

The owners of the pubs, Bass Taverns Limited and Samuel Smith Breweries, had little reason to move. Both pubs were performing well in their current location and, in February 1997, eight months after the bomb, had reopened. Another sticking point was that both buildings were listed. They could not simply be torn down and moved in a couple of days – that would have been illegal. Sinclair's was a Grade II building, while the Old Wellington was Grade II* and also a Scheduled Ancient Monument. English Heritage, among others, would need to be convinced, and planning applications would need to be submitted and approved.

As if all this was not enough it would, quite remarkably, be the second time in 25 years that the buildings had been moved. Back in 1974 they were raised by 1.5m to fit in with the Shambles Square Market Place development and to align with the altered street levels and underground vehicular access.

After much negotiation, both obstacles were overcome. The breweries agreed to the relocation of the pubs, so long as their new location, 200m north at the junction of Cathedral Gates and Cateaton Street and adjacent to the Corn Exchange, met certain design criteria that would not adversely affect trading. Secondly, the town planning applications that were submitted (one to 'dismantle' both pubs and one to re-erect) were dealt with promptly (submitted 30 June 1997 and approved 23 September 1997).

It was not a completely smooth process. Concerns were raised by the breweries during the planning process, mainly due to a proposed 3.6m-high Belvedere railing wall which would terminate the north end of New Cathedral Street, thereby potentially compromising their commercial viability and long-term future. In seeking to ameliorate such concerns, Howard Bernstein advised both breweries in writing on 15 July 1997 that a solution would be found:

'You can have my complete assurance that the Breweries will be fully consulted in the way these proposals are developed in detail. Their agreement will be sought prior to any amendment being brought to the planning authority for formal determination.'

Amendments to the design were agreed and the applications approved. The pubs could, for the second time in their history, be moved.

▲ Old Wellington and Sinclair's Oyster Bar, 1997.

▲▼ Old Wellington and Sinclair's Oyster Bar before and during construction of Shambles Square.

▲▼ Buttress Fuller Alsop Williams's record of the Old Wellington and Sinclair's Oyster Bar.

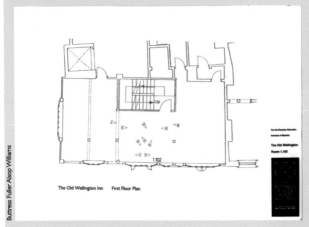

Contractor Watkin Jones Construction was appointed to manage the dismantling of the pubs at Shambles Square. Manchester based architects with specialist expertise in the conservation and restoration of historical buildings, Buttress Fuller Alsop Williams, were responsible for the task of meticulously labelling, recording, measuring and photographing every single joint, peg and piece of timber in both pubs (in total over 10,000 items) – a condition of the planning approval. This way, like pieces of Mecano, the pubs could be dismantled and reconstructed in their new location as accurately as possible (literally, piece by piece). It was vital that the reconstruction was authentic and faithfully reproduced 'wear and tear'. This included tobacco stains on the ceiling, uneven floors and gaps between oak beams.

The new site, which was outlined in the Edaw masterplan, had previously been home to a shop and, in the past, a school of motoring. Plans for its redevelopment had been in place years before the bomb, with planning permission granted in 1992 for a new four-storey office building (eerily granted on 15 June 1992 – exactly four years before the bomb). When the bomb went off, the landowners, Manchester Cathedral, still had a year in which to implement the planning permission. Consequently, the building could (and would) be demolished immediately.

The pubs were re-assembled in their new location and opened for trade in September 1999. In the years that have followed they have become an intrinsic part of Exchange Square and Manchester city centre.

▼ The Old Wellington and Sinclair's Oyster Bar.

Buttress Fuller Alsop Williams

Buttress Fuller Alsop Williams

Buttress Fuller Alsop Williams

It is fascinating to point out that The Old Wellington and Sinclair's are not the only pubs that have been physically moved before in Manchester city centre. At 16 Fountain Street, just off Market Street, visitors can find a pub called 'The Shakespeare'. Remarkably this building actually dates from 1656, and used to be 'The Shambles Inn' in Chester. In 1928 the building was dismantled and transported to Manchester and reassembled in its present form by architects Johnson, W. A. & Sons. According to the plaque on the side of the building, it is suggested that the pub is haunted by the ghost of a girl who died in the pub over 100 years ago when it was located in Chester.

▲ Dismantling the Old Wellington.

Buttress Fuller Alsop Williams

▼ The Old Wellington and Sinclair's Oyster Bar.

© Aidan O'Rourke - www.aidan.co.uk

▼▲ Rebuilding the Old Wellington and Sinclair's Oyster Bar.

Buttress Fuller Alsop Williams

▼ The Shakespeare, Fountain Street.

© Evan Kellie

Aside from the bomb-damaged area, what has happened elsewhere in the city centre, and how has Manchester City Council sought to balance new development at all scales with the protection of its heritage?

WORKING WITH LISTED BUILDINGS

The city was home in the early part of the new millennium to some excellent conversions and restorations of historic buildings. One of the first pieces of restoration that was completed in the years following the bomb was that of the six-storey Grade II listed Joshua Hoyle Warehouse at 38–50 Piccadilly, located within the designated Piccadilly Gateway and immediately opposite what would become Piccadilly Place.

The building was constructed in 1904 by Charles Heathcote and, like many buildings of its type, had stood idle and fallen into disuse and disrepair. Forming part of the Piccadilly Regeneration Study, issued in 1997, the sensitive refurbishment of the building into a four-star 120-bed Malmaison Hotel, by Darby Associates, was completed in 1998. The work sought to capture the essence of the hotel chain in terms of comfort and style and included the demolition of the warehouse interior while retaining the front elevation façade. A further extension to the rear was completed in 2001. Without question, it represented a considerable improvement to the important corner of Piccadilly and Auburn Street.

Smithfield Buildings on Tib Street, in the Northern Quarter, is another excellent example. The property had seen several changes of ownership in the 30-year period up to development. Following the closure of department store Affleck & Brown, the property became British Home Stores, then Littlewoods, both of which relocated to the Arndale Centre during the early 1970s. British property developers, Urban Splash, founded by Tom Bloxham MBE and Jonathan Falkingham, acquired the building in the mid-1990s and appointed architects Stephenson Bell to introduce innovative design solutions.

Construction began in late 1995 and was completed in March 1998. The development introduced 81 loft-style apartments, along with 21 retail units. Its success was mirrored by its inclusion in the Urban Task Force Report 'Towards a Strong Urban Renaissance' published by members of The Urban Task Force, chaired by Lord Rodgers, in June 1999. The report, which introduced the scheme under the heading 'pioneering urban living in the north west', stated that quality had been achieved on three 'levels': in heritage terms as a 'recycling job' within a conservation area; urbanistically as a perimeter block that cleverly provides active frontage on all sides; and stylistically as a chic piece of contemporary design.

Innovative and sensitive conversions and refurbishment took place across all parts of the city centre. In May 2000, the city council approved an application that sought to convert the vacant Church of St George on Arundel Street into 25 residential units. Designed by architects Makin Architecture, the scheme is a wonderful, sensitive conversion.

During the period of 2004 to 2007 the John Rylands Library – a Grade 1 listed building on Deansgate – was closed for refurbishment. The building, which is owned by the University of Manchester, had begun to deteriorate structurally by the late 1990s, causing concern over the collections held inside and leading to the refurbishment project. The project was led by architects Austin-Smith:Lord and was completed in September 2007.

▲ Malmaison.

▼ Smithfield Buildings.

◄ Former St George's Church, Chester Road.

Ian Lawson Photography

Ian Lawson Photography

◄ John Rylands Library.

REBUILDING MANCHESTER

▲ CIS Tower.

▲▼ Solar panels added to the CIS Tower.

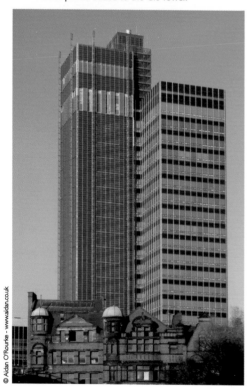

Such work was not limited to pre-war listed buildings. The 25-storey CIS Tower, designed by G.S. Hay of the CWS and Gordon Tait of Sir John Burnet, Tait & Partners and constructed between 1959 and 1962, is Manchester city centre's only listed post-war building (designated in 1995). In March 2003 planning permission was granted by Manchester City Council, allowing the re-cladding of the service tower in glazed photovoltaic panels – the largest solar project of its kind ever undertaken in Europe. By 2005 the scheme, valued at £5.5 million, was complete with 7,000 blue solar panels in place, generating 180,000 units of electricity each year. On 3 November 2005 Prime Minister Tony Blair completed the project by switching on the panels.

The protection of listed buildings has also formed part of so many of Manchester's small-scale and comprehensive redevelopments as presented elsewhere in the book: The People's History Museum at Spinningfields, Carvers's Warehouse and Jackson's Warehouse at Piccadilly Basin, Chetham's School of Music, part of the Medieval Quarter in the northern end of the city and so many of the buildings in Castlefield. Equally, Bruntwood, as presented in the 'Commercial' chapter, has refurbished so many tired post-war historic buildings. But it has not been straightforward. The Free Trade Hall is a case in point.

▲▼ The People's History Museum.　Austin-Smith: Lord

▲ Chetham's School of Music.

Austin-Smith: Lord

► Free Trade Hall, Peter Street.

The Free Trade Hall

Undoubtedly one of the greatest heritage challenges in Manchester city centre – and one of the most high profile – has been that of the Grade II* listed Free Trade Hall on Peter Street. The building, and the site itself, has a special place in Manchester's history. It was where the Peterloo Massacre took place in 1819, in which 60,000 had gathered at a meeting to demand the reform of parliamentary representation, and 11 people were killed and 140 injured. The Free Trade Hall was constructed in 1856 by distinguished Victorian architect Edwards Walters and replaced the first hall on the site which had been built in 1840. Over the years it would be the venue for plays, meetings, concerts and events; a place where figureheads such as Churchill, Disraeli, Lloyd George and Gladstone would share their thoughts and also a place that hosted gentlemen such as Charles Dickens and Oscar Wilde. It would also be home to the Halle Orchestra for 138 years.

It was almost completely destroyed as a result of the Blitz in World War Two. When the hall was rebuilt to a new design in 1951 – the first building in the city centre to be rebuilt – only the outer shell of the Peter Street and Southmill Street frontages were retained. There was no surviving interior element of the Victorian structure, but it was still viewed by some as the epicentre of Manchester – captured by the editor of the *Manchester Evening News* following its reopening by the Queen (wife of George VI) on November 16 1951:

'Henceforward the Free Trade Hall will be the centre and setting of the teeming manifestations of Manchester's life. It will be the centre of our city insomuch as our musical, cultural, educational, political and social life will converge upon it. If Manchester has a soul here it may be found; and God grant that it will become the centre and bulwark of every kind of cause that lifts up the people and ennobles a city. The bombs that Hilter's emissaries rained down on the old Hall seemed to extinguish an altar flame in the city. Now it burns again and there is a deep stirring of pride in our hearts.'

Post-war, it was Manchester's contribution to the Festival of Britain in 1951, and notably American singer Bob Dylan performed twice at the Hall, in 1965 and 1966. According to the fascinating *The Hall of Fame: A History of the Free Trade Hall*, published by Radisson Edwardian in 2004 to mark the opening of the new hotel, Dylan's second performance was noteworthy, to say the least:

'…the concert was to become one of the most admired and discussed live performances in modern pop music, made all the more riveting by the slow handclapping and barracking from sections of the audience and the cry of "Judas" as Dylan sang that "something was happening but you don't know what it is".'

During 1976 the Sex Pistols played at the 'Lesser Free Trade Hall' a total of four times. This included the gig on 4th June 1976, considered by many to be one of the most influential concerts of all time. Attendees included Joy Division, soon-to-be Smiths vocalist Morrissey and Factory Records-founder Anthony H. Wilson – all of whom went on to cite the concert as an inspiration in their own musical endeavours.

► Sex Pistols advert.

▲ Vision for the redevelopment of the Free Trade Hall.

▼ 'Sold', Free Trade Hall, April 2002.

The use of the building as a concern hall ceased in August 1996 when the Halle Orchestra relocated to the Bridgewater Hall. The building, which was owned by Manchester City Council, was placed for sale on the open market. Developers Beazer were shortlisted and selected in January 1990. The process then was to choose an appropriate use for the building based upon need, sustainability and deliverability. The only use that met the criteria was that of a hotel. Following marketing and discussions, two proposals were submitted by developers to Manchester City Council for the conversion of the Free Trade Hall for hotel purposes. Beazer, who by this time had been taken over by Hanson plc, refined their proposals but eventually could not commit to any development of the Hall.

Consultants and engineers AMEC became involved at the invitation of Beazer. Consequently, AMEC introduced La Sander (NW) Limited to Manchester City Council, and in 1993 they were appointed as preferred developer for the hall. The proposals that were eventually prepared complemented a planning brief that had been produced by CMDC in 1995.

A planning application was subsequently submitted in April 1997 for a 291-bedroom, five-star hotel with a 16-storey building erected to the rear (the façade on Peter Street would be retained). Irrespective of any architectural quality, the application generated much furore in the city. The *Manchester Metro News* announced on 27 June 1997 that more than 4,000 people had signed a petition opposing the proposed development. Despite the city council recommending approval of the scheme, a public inquiry was announced by then Environment Secretary John Prescott in October 1997. Speaking to the *Manchester Evening News* on 22 October 1997, city leader Councillor Richard Leese outlined his frustration with the decision:

'This is appalling news. Over the past 10 years a search for new uses for the hall have come to nothing. English Heritage and the Civic Society have completely ignored the years of work that have gone into trying to find alternative uses. The current hall is not the original building. Only two walls remain, the rest is a reconstruction following war time bombing.'

In the build up to the inquiry an independent architectural advisor, Anthony Blee, was appointed by the city council to give consideration to design issues. Following this the original application was withdrawn and a revised scheme was subsequently submitted for planning approval on February 1998, proposing a taller building that would take the height to 24 storeys. The application once again attracted significant levels of opposition, including a vehement objection from English Heritage.

▶ Radisson Hotel.

◀ Radisson Hotel.

The public inquiry, which considered the revised scheme, was held in April 1998. Six months later – an indication of the potentially lengthy timescales involved – on 8 October 1998 John Prescott announced his decision to refuse the scheme, declaring it in his view to be 'fundamentally flawed', while the size and position of the new build elements would dominate the retained Victorian façades. From a strategic perspective it cast light on the challenges faced by any city seeking to secure regeneration and investment while also bringing important historic buildings back into use. In the same article *The Economist*, in an article published on 15 October 1998, warned the city council that in their 'rush to build a shiny new post-industrial future, Manchester is in danger of neglecting its potentially valuable past.'

Once the dust had settled following the decision, Manchester City Council went on to re-market the building in close consultation with English Heritage. A scheme submitted by La Sandre and designed by architects Stephenson Bell was selected. In 2000 a new application was submitted, again for a hotel, with a 16-storey element to the rear along Windmill Street. Following recommendation for approval at Manchester City Council Planning Committee on 23 November 2000, further modifications were made to the design of the scheme. Planning permission was eventually granted, construction began in 2002 and the Radisson Hotel opened in 2004. An indication of the success of the final scheme was the inclusion of the project within English Heritage's 2006 book, *Shared Interest*. Robert Evans, Associate Director at architects Stephenson Bell, was complimentary:

'English Heritage was approachable and constructive from the outset of the design process and allowed a good working relationship to be established. Such consultation established broad principles and parameters for Stephenson Bell to work within.'

DEVELOPMENT IN CONSERVATION AREAS

The challenge of encouraging and approving development in conservation areas is not limited to just new or modified buildings. It also controls the demolition of unlisted buildings. In many cases when dealing with such processes the city council has adopted the stance of delivering 'the bigger picture' (captured by the Commercial Chambers story – see 'Space and Connectivity').

The story of Northcliffe House provides a useful starting point. Five storeys high and previously located in the Deansgate and Peter Street conservation area on the west side of Deansgate at its corner with Hardman Street, the building was completed in 1932 and had been vacant since 1989 when the Daily Mail newspaper editorial and printing facility closed and relocated to Trafford Park. While the building was not listed, several parties wanted the building to be retained and form part of the Spinningfields masterplan. In any event, it was within a conservation area so planning permission would be needed to demolish the building.

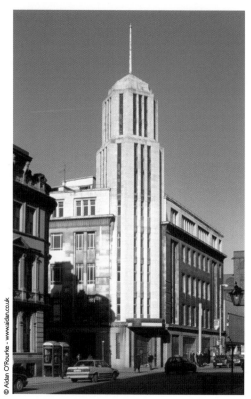

▲ Northcliffe House, Deansgate.

Consequently, a planning application was submitted by architects Sheppard Robson in 2001, seeking permission for a new office building for the Royal Bank of Scotland and also to demolish Northcliffe House. In determining the application, the city council's view was one of 'looking at the bigger picture', as outlined by the 13 December 2001 Planning Committee Report:

'After considering the quality of Northcliffe House and the contribution it makes to the local scene, the condition of the building and the cost of its retention, the efforts which have been made to bring the building back into use, the likelihood of any scheme being brought forward which would retain the existing building shell, the quality of the proposed replacement building, the function it would perform and its role as a flagship scheme in a much wider regeneration initiative, the demolition is considered to be justified.'

Permission was granted, and during 2002 the building was demolished.

Another scheme that would make the city council balance investment and preservation came in December 2006 at the height of the economic boom. A scheme proposed by Manchester and Metropolitan Properties and designed by architects Squire and Partners comprised over 230,000sq ft (20,000m^2) of office space within a 14-storey building and was located on land occupied by an Odeon Cinema, which had closed in 2004 and remained vacant since. Like Northcliffe House, the building was not listed but fell within the George Street conservation area and adjacent to the St Peter's Street and Deansgate / Peter Street conservation area.

Concerns were raised during the process by a number of third parties, including the Cinema Theatres Association, who wrote to English Heritage and proposed that the building be 'spotlisted' to safeguard it from demolition. Even more vociferous were the city council's Conservation Areas and Historic Buildings Panel, who noted the importance of the Odeon building and its uniqueness within Manchester's 'entertainment' corridor.

The city council, when determining the application in February 2007, did not share such concerns. Once again, the focus was on the 'bigger picture' and the drive to deliver a scheme that would bring city-wide regeneration benefits – something

▼ Odeon Cinema, Oxford Road.

Squire and Partners

Squire and Partners

▲ Landmark Manchester, Oxford Road.

that was of particular importance bearing in mind the site's presence within the northern end of 'Corridor Manchester': a strategic link stretching from St Peter's Square to Whitworth Park forming a backbone to the city's 'knowledge' economy.

Let us be clear, however, that the city council has not approved every single proposal that has been submitted. There are many schemes that have not made it into the public arena because the council has told the applicant/architect during confidential discussions that the proposal is not good enough or in the right location – sometimes both. There are others that have made it to the application stage. There are two to consider. The first is the proposal at Jacksons Wharf in Castlefield – this is presented in the 'Residential' chapter.

▲   Space Developments site, Rochdale Road.

The second is a proposal by Space Developments on land at 13–17 Rochdale Road, just north of the city centre. The proposals, which were submitted in February 2008, sought consent for a part 15, part 13 and part 10-storey building consisting of 134 apartments on a piece of vacant land. Despite the inevitable regeneration benefits that would have come from the proposed development, Manchester City Council officers in their Planning Committee Report published on 24 July 2008 considered that the 'negative aspects/effects of the scheme outweigh the positive effects.' Consequently, the scheme was refused permission in July 2008.

The applicants appealed.

The Planning Inspectorate, however, shared the view of the city council. While the site was not located in a conservation area, it was considered by the inspectorate that the building could be viewed from the nearby Smithfield conservation area. In addition, although it was not adjacent to any listed buildings, the CIS Tower was only a short walk away and other listed buildings of smaller scale exist in the nearby Angel Meadows.

CONCLUSION

Manchester City Council, in its drive to secure investment and regeneration and improve the quality of life for the people of Manchester, has had to try and balance conservation and preservation of the built environment with that of new buildings and spaces. This has required some difficult decisions. The story is largely one of success but with trials and tribulations along the way – most notably the Free Trade Hall. But then, the story is about how the city council learnt from this experience and how it created processes and partnerships, particularly with English Heritage, to try and make sure the same mistakes did not happen again.

The 'dynamic' approach displayed by the use of 'façadism' in conservation areas, such as The Printworks, along with the relocation of the Shambles pubs has been the right one when, as former Leader Graham Stringer once said, cities cannot afford to stand still. It is all about finding a balance, considering the bigger picture, and delivering the greater good. Some of the work in the late 1970s and early 1980s was, and still is, inspirational: GMEX, Museum of Science and Industry and the Royal Exchange.

The future continues to look bright. There are some wonderful individual buildings and areas that still need attention (such as the vacant Fire Station on London Road) along with parts of St Peter's Square. Plans are already in place, and it is difficult not to feel confident that the council will continue to work in partnership and make the most of Manchester's unique historic character.

▲   Princess Street and Kennedy Street buildings, 1998.

41–51 Princess Street and 28–36 Kennedy Street

In the same vein as the Free Trade Hall proposals, the city council has come up against problems in respect of proposals in conservation areas, as well as sensitive listed buildings.

Closer to home (quite literally, opposite the Town Hall and the city council offices) there was, up until 2003, a real eyesore in Manchester city centre. Buildings at 41–51 Princess Street and 28–36 Kennedy Street, owned at the time by former Lord Mayor Sir Neil Westbrook, had been vacant since the late 1980s and, consequently, had deteriorated very badly. It had not gone unnoticed – particularly by the *Evening News*, who had held a campaign for their development.

To the city council's relief, a scheme for the site was prepared and submitted in January 1998 which sought to demolish the buildings and replace them with an eight-storey office building. As with the Free Trade Hall, the scheme attracted levels of opposition and once again, despite the city council supporting the proposals, a public inquiry was held. Environment Secretary John Prescott sided once again with the opponents and refused the scheme on 16 June 1999. The proposals were, in his mind, out of scale and out of character with the Albert Square and Upper King Street conservation areas. In an article published by the *Estates Gazette* on 28 June 1999, Winston Parr of Manchester Civic Society said his relief at the decision 'goes beyond parochial joy over our treasured buildings'.

▼   The rear of 55 Kennedy Street.

The refusal delayed the process and the derelict buildings were given a stay of execution. Like the Free Trade Hall, the message was clear: work with, rather than against, English Heritage and a solution will be found.

It was not until mid-2003 when the site was sold to Stockport-based property company CTP that fresh proposals could be prepared. The scheme this time was designed by architects Hodder Associates (now 'Hodder + Partners'). The proposals for a slightly lower office building, which had been prepared in close consultation with English Heritage, were submitted in October 2003 and approved in March 2004. Finally, the derelict properties could be cleared.

The new building called Aurora (dubbed by CTP as 'the building of light') opened in late 2006.

▶   View towards 55 Princess Street, designed by Hodder Associates.

'From haute couture to high street...
Shops in Manchester have it all, all
within a neat square mile.'

– www.visitmanchester.com

RETAIL

BEFORE THE BOMB

The quality of the shopping experience in Manchester city centre has been a priority for the city council for years – recognition that a strong retail offering attracts people, vitality and vibrancy.

World War Two played a crucial role in establishing the retail core in the city centre which, for many years, had revolved around markets and stalls. Many of the shopping facilities, located on Oldham Street at that time, were badly damaged during the Blitz in 1940, and consequently many buildings were demolished. In the years that followed, the traditional retail circuit which was centred around Lewis's and Paulden's department stores at the eastern end of Market Street and along Oldham Street, where stores such as C&A, Modes and Affleck and Brown were to be found, became noticeably unattractive and congested. In addition to the qualitative decline, the frustrations of parking restrictions imposed in the city centre drove car-bound shoppers away to satellite towns in Greater Manchester, and elsewhere in the region.

Consistent with many of the projects introduced in the book, Manchester City Council took control of the situation and aimed high. A 'Comprehensive Development Area' was subsequently identified and allocated in the early 1960s. This swallowed up much of the land bound by High Street, Market Street, Corporation Street and Shudehill. The goal behind this approach was to clear many of the vacant and poor-quality buildings (similar in many respects to the aspirations of the 1945 Plan) and provide an upgraded and enhanced retail core – something that would attract new shops and make the city centre a more exciting, vibrant place to visit. The 1967 City Centre Map set out the objective:

'The fact that much of the shopping centre is obsolete and substandard suggests that whatever the ultimate position, considerable redevelopment and replacement is essential to maintain and improve its position as a centre of attraction. The pattern of the shopping centre needs reshaping and advantage taken of the opportunity to provide good car parking facilities for the motorist shopper, more convenient access to public transport, and safe and inviting conditions for the pedestrian.'

REBUILDING **MANCHESTER**

Arndale Developments

The Arndale Centre in Manchester is not the only one – not by any means. Here are some interesting facts:

The word 'Arndale' was derived from the names of the two Yorkshire-based businessmen who established the company: Arnold Hagenbach ('Arn') and Sam Chippindale ('Dale').

The first centre was opened in Jarrow in 1961.

In total, 22 Arndale Centres have been built in the UK.

The centres typically appeared in towns and cities where the retail experience was moribund.

Many of the centres have since been renamed (for example in Leeds and Poole).

With this framework and mechanism in place the retail offer, along with Manchester city centre's cityscape, changed beyond recognition. It was during this period that a name, still present in Manchester, appeared on the scene. Arndale Developments of Bradford had been buying sites across the UK since 1952 and, in line with the Comprehensive Development Area allocation outlined by Manchester City Council, submitted a major scheme for the site in 1965. Leading architects of the time Wilson and Womersley, who were very much in favour with Manchester City Council having already designed the University Precinct on Oxford Road, were appointed by Arndale Developments to design what would become the largest covered shopping centre in Europe: The Arndale Centre.

The brief, issued by Arndale Developments to Wilson and Womersley, sought to deliver a shopping centre based upon the principles of an American mall – in other words, using large stores with strong branding (in this instance Littlewoods and British Home Stores) as landmarks so people visit subsidiary stores while navigating between the larger units. Architecturally, the centre would be considered 'inward-looking' with a dark underground bus station and little pedestrian connectivity with the rest of Manchester city centre and its surrounding streets – something that the city council had encouraged as part of the design process:

'A major condition of planning approval was the restriction of shopping frontage on all the perimeter streets and Cannon Street, except for Market Street itself and the immediate returns on Corporation and High Street.'

Following the granting of planning permission, construction of the centre commenced in 1973, in conjunction with another major shopping development known as the Shambles Square Market Place, located at the northern end of Deansgate. The Arndale would, in the end, cost an astonishing £100 million to build – the equivalent of approximately £500 million in 2010 prices.

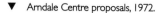
▼ Arndale Centre proposals, 1972.

▼ Market Street vision – taken from the 1967 City Centre Map.

▶ Vision for the Arndale Centre – taken from the 1967 City Centre Map.

Manchester Archives and Local Studies

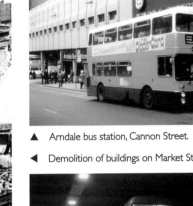

▲ Arndale bus station, Cannon Street.

◀ Demolition of buildings on Market Street, 1973.

▲ Inside the Arndale bus station.

The self-contained nature of the scheme, which included on-site car parking and integration with the bus station, meant that a visitor could enter the building directly by bus or car and leave without seeing the rest of the city centre, let alone the exterior of the building. Upon its completion in 1978, critics were quick to pour scorn on the building from both and architectural and functional perspective. Author Richard J. Williams, in his book *The Anxious City*, described the centre as a 'godless retail mall.'

The exterior was also subject to much criticism. Most of the centre was covered by pre-cast concrete panels, faced with ceramic tiles. Many individuals have claimed that they came up with the infamous title of the world's largest gent's toilet. Perhaps it peaked in 1995 when the reference was used by acclaimed author Bill Bryson in his book *Notes from a Small Island*. In an interview published by *The Guardian* on 16 October 1978, architect Kenneth Shone of Wilson and Womersley outlined his disappointment with the general reaction – both in terms of the scale of the demolition to clear the site and also to the buildings appearance:

'I think it's a bit rough now for people to start knocking [Sam] Chippendale or us because in the meantime the tide has turned. Conservation has become the in-thing, as if conservatism and redevelopment were mutually exclusive. We did what we did in good faith.'

Despite the foibles of the design, it was a commercial success, something that was recognised by the *Manchester Evening News* on 27 June 1978 who reported that the Arndale Centre had provided the city with,

▼ Arndale Centre and Shudehill – Cromford Court apartments visible in the top left.

REBUILDING **MANCHESTER**

▲ Arndale Centre's famous tiles – still in use in places in 2010.

in financial terms, a 'generous blood transfusion'. Indeed the Arndale Centre and the Shambles Square Market Place had together brought the city centre some 1,560,000sq ft (145,000m^2) of new shopping floorspace. This was a huge – the same size as the Trafford Centre!

Improvements were implemented elsewhere by way of pedestrianisation, eliminating traffic and introducing paved open space. King Street was the first in 1975. It was evident at the time that other parts of the city centre needed urgent attention. On 29 January 1975 the *Evening News* published an article, entitled 'chaos in St Ann's Square', drawing attention to traffic and congestion and the general lapse in environmental quality. In 1984 St Ann's Square was also pedestrianised and enhanced considerably.

Despite all this hard work, the city centre retail market continued to struggle as the recession of the late 1970s began to bite. A review of shopping trends published in *The Guardian* on 23 February 1983 questioned Manchester's strength as a shopping destination. One way or another it was slipping down the league table:

'City centre traders maintain that over the last 15 years Manchester has gone from being the number one provincial trading city to somewhere between twelfth and thirteenth. In many cases the stores in Manchester city centre are the largest outside London, but frequently the sales turnovers is below that of smaller shops not only in other cities such as Liverpool, Birmingham and Leeds, but also in large towns such as Dunfermline and Southport.'

Things were about to become more difficult. Manchester faced a new challenge in the 1980s with the growth of out-of-town shopping centres. A detailed study prepared by consultants Roger Tym & Partners in late 1986 (commissioned by the Association of Greater Manchester Authorities) considered the possible effects of schemes in Greater Manchester

▼ St Ann's Square, before and after pedestrianisation.

that proposed nearly 3,000,000sq ft (278,000m²) of new development, all in out-of-centre locations. Schemes under the spotlight included: two proposals at Barton Lock and Kingsway, both in excess of 600,000sq ft (55,700m²); the 667,000sq ft (62,000m²) Manchester Ship Canal Co. project at Dumplington (now know as The Trafford Centre); and plans by Spring Park Securities for a 372,000sq ft (35,000m²) development at Woodford.

The report concluded that if all 10 major schemes went ahead, the potential impact on Manchester city centre was the loss of trade worth £33 million – big figures indeed. The conclusion, outlined in *The Estates Gazette* on 24 January 1987, was clear:

'Central Manchester has only recently emerged from a period of relative instability, and rental levels are just beginning to rise to a level which is more appropriate to its size and importance. At present the regional centre [Manchester] would find it difficult to withstand successfully the scale of impacts calculated...without experiencing an increase in vacancies in fringe retail positions.'

The message was simple: action was needed. Accordingly, the *Manchester Evening News* on 9 December 1989 announced a £9 million refurbishment planned for the Arndale Centre (the headline was quite bold: 'a shiny new face for the ugly Arndale'). The proposals included some aesthetic improvements with a glazed façade which would overlook Market Street, thus minimising the impact of the tiles.

The changes certainly had a positive impact. By 1991 there were two very distinct areas for shoppers in the city centre; the heartland of Market Street and the Arndale Centre, hosting big names such as Boots, Argos and HMV.

▼ King Street, before and after pedestrianisation.

Manchester Archives and Local Studies

© Aidan O'Rourke - www.aidan.co.uk

REBUILDING **MANCHESTER**

In addition there were the more picturesque, fashionable shopping areas along King Street and in St Ann's Square (anchored by the Royal Exchange Shopping Centre and Barton Arcade) providing a link with St Mary's Gate and back into Market Street. People were starting to spend time, and money, in Manchester. Moreover, the perception of the city-centre retail offer was much stronger.

Despite this improvement, Manchester City Council refused to settle back. Their objective, quite the opposite, was set out in the 1994 City Pride prospectus:

'To put Manchester on a level with European cities, the range and quality of retail provision must be developed to achieve international standards. A new development within the central zone is critical and will be designed to expand the provision of speciality shopping as well as to contribute to the repopulation of the centre and improve the range and quality of existing retail provision.'

Just as everything was starting to look rosy, a new challenge appeared on the horizon. In 1995, following a lengthy and expensive appeal process, the proposed Trafford Centre at Dumplington was granted planning permission. Construction could now commence, and very soon shoppers would have a major alternative to Manchester city centre.

▶ Marks & Spencer (Market Street), junction of Market Street and Corporation Street, Manchester, 1961.

▼ Marks & Spencer, Corporation Street, 1963.

Manchester Archives and Local Studies

Manchester Archives and Local Studies

One of the most important retail anchors in the city centre at this time was the Marks & Spencer store, located on the axis of Corporation Street and Cross Street, opposite the Arndale Centre. The store opened in 1962 adjacent to the Market Place area (the site of Manchester's medieval market place), a move which contributed to a more compact and continuous shopping pattern in the city centre by providing a pivot between Market Street and St Ann's Square. The new store also comprised a six-storey office block above, known as Michael House. It went on to become their fourth-largest store in the country and was also their administration centre for the North West.

Ironically, just weeks before the 15 June 1996 Marks & Spencer had been in discussions with Manchester City Council in respect of extending their store on Corporation Street. As outlined by University of Manchester lecturer Gwyndaf Williams in his book *Enterprising the City*, it is understood preliminary discussions had also taken place with Royal Insurance regarding the possible procurement of the adjacent Longridge House office building. In an interview with the *Manchester Evening News* published on 11 July 1997 Roger Aldridge who, at the time, was main board director responsible for estates and store development for Marks & Spencer made it clear that the store had limited future potential:

'Over the last 10–15 years, we have regularly carried out extensions and improvements, but Manchester was not an easy site to develop. The first floor was very long and, at its extremity, had inadequate links from below. I'd had meetings with planners seven weeks before the explosion about what we might do next. The bomb was a terrible occurrence but what it has done is give us a chance to expand.'

The bomb, of course, devastated the store along with hundreds of other shop units in the city centre.

AFTER THE BOMB

The devastation brought with it an unprecedented opportunity for Manchester City Council and the Manchester Millennium Task Force to significantly enhance and remodel the city's retail experience – something that had been on the task list for years. It was an opportunity to diversify; to make Manchester a shopping experience for everyone. There were four landmark retail schemes (as well as 'The Printworks', although this is predominantly a leisure-based destination – see 'Leisure' chapter for more).

MARKS & SPENCER

Providing Marks & Spencer with a new store was the centrepiece of the Edaw masterplan. The replacement building, designed by BDP, would replace the original store as well as land immediately adjacent, previously occupied by the Longridge House office building. The new building would bring with it 250,000sq ft (23,225m^2) of space – treble the size of the store devastated by the blast. At the time it would be the largest Marks & Spencer in the world.

As a result of the mechanisms put in place by the city council and the task force, introduced in the 'Saturday 15 June 1996' chapter, action was prompt. The planning application for the new store was one of the first to be submitted to the city council and was received on Christmas Eve 1996 – only six months after the bomb had been detonated. The

MARKS & SPENCER

As outlined by the *Manchester Evening News* on 11 June 1997, Marks & Spencer has always had deep-rooted connections with Manchester:

The city was home to their first shop, located at 20 Cheetham Hill Road. It was also the childhood home of Simon Marks, the company's longest-serving chairman.

The company opened its second store in the city in 1896 at 63 Stretford Road.

A year later, their first warehouse was set up on Robert Street near Strangeways.

In 1901 their warehouse in Manchester became their first registered address and headquarters.

Two years later, they became a Limited Company, with each founder having half of the capital of 30,000 £1 shares.

In 1924 they relocated the company headquarters to London.

REBUILDING **MANCHESTER**

▶ Marks & Spencer store on its first day of trading, 25 November 1999.

▼ Cleared Marks & Spencer site.

Stephen Welsh

▼ Marks & Spencer under construction.

Stephen Welsh

▼ Workers on Corporation Street, with the Marks & Spencer building rising in the background.

Stephen Welsh

need for prompt delivery in these exceptional circumstances (enhanced further by the impending opening of The Trafford Centre and the hosting of the Commonwealth Games in 2002) was recognised by all parties who played a role in the determination of the planning application. This ethos was mirrored by English Heritage in a letter to Manchester City Council on 27 January 1997:

'It is not normally considered acceptable to entertain an outline application for a site of such importance which is so prominent in the city centre conservation area and so close to groups of historic buildings. However the circumstances of the loss of these buildings leads us not to raise objections to the application provided that the details of the redevelopment will be conditioned in accordance with the City Council's anticipated SPG for the Bomb Damaged Area.'

By June 1997, a year after the blast, both the old Marks & Spencer building and the adjacent Longridge House office building had been demolished and the site was clear. Over the next two and a half years, hundreds of people worked tirelessly on the site and behind the scenes, making sure that the new store would be delivered in time for the new millennium.

The new store, as promised, was delivered on time and opened to the public on Thursday 25 November 1999. In an article published by *The Independent* on the same day, Howard Bernstein reiterated the vision from day one:

'It was crucial that our predominant role as the retail and business centre of the region might not be threatened. From the start it was decided not merely to repair...but turn the adversity into an opportunity to replan.'

In September 2002 Selfridges moved into the northern part of the Marks & Spencer building, taking up 120,000sq ft of space (11,148m²). This was a further landmark addition to Manchester's retail offering.

ARNDALE CENTRE

One of the greatest opportunities that came from the bomb was the chance to address the appearance and functionality of the Arndale Centre. This was recognised by all parties. In an interview that appeared on the BBC programme *Close Up North* in October 1996, architect Ian Simpson, whose practice formed part of the Edaw team, was very clear about the challenge:

'The Arndale Centre is, as it stands, atrocious. The bulk of the Arndale really needs re-skinning, not with a cladding but with a new building form and that's what we are intending; to put new buildings along the edges of the Arndale that have a different use – maybe residential at the upper levels – but have a street frontage and to face out rather than inwards'

Manchester City Council agreed. Their guidance for the bomb-damaged area emphasised the need for quality:

'The physical remodelling and significant upgrading of the Arndale Centre will provide major, improved, shopping provision of high quality; a greatly upgraded environment to Withy Grove; and increased complementary facilities for shoppers and other visitors enabling Manchester City Centre to continue to develop as a major retail centre and European city. It will provide the opportunity for the Arndale Centre to be much more outward looking and make a much greater contribution to on street shopping provision, particularly on Corporation Street/Cross Street and Withy Grove.'

In rebuilding and enhancing the Arndale Centre there were therefore two objectives that would be delivered hand-in-hand over a series of years. First and foremost, the exterior of the building needed to be improved. Piece by piece, the tiled façade along Cross Street and Corporation Street was stripped and reclad between 1996 and 1999. This was followed in the new millennium by enhancements to the majority of the Market Street façades.

The second objective was to greatly enhance the shopping experience within the Arndale Centre. The southern portion, adjacent to Market Street, was generally successful and trading well. It was the northern element that needed considerable work. Prudential had secured a controlling interest in the centre as of March 1998 and were keen to appoint a design team to look at the opportunities. In an interview published by *FX Magazine* in October 2000 Prudential's Development Director, John Weymouth, was clear about the challenge:

'Many of the existing units no longer suit modern retail requirements, and the internal pedestrian flows and entrances can be confusing to follow and difficult to find. Our proposals both respond to the [masterplan] and extend it with the creation of retail opportunities.'

The proposals, designed by architects Chapman Taylor, were big. Valued at £125 million, the work would be delivered in three phases and meet the broad objectives established by the Edaw masterplan set out in 1996. Once complete, the work would

▲ Alterations to the Arndale Centre frontage on Market Street, September 2002.

▲ Arndale Centre, Corporation Street, before the bomb.

▼▶ Arndale Centre, Cross Street.

REBUILDING **MANCHESTER**

▶ The cleared northern section of the Arndale Centre site with the Corn Exchange in background, along with Urbis and Printworks.

Stephen Welsh

bring 500,000sq ft (46,450m²) of new and replacement retail space to Manchester city centre. The scheme would improve the Arndale and the city centre aesthetically and in terms of connectivity by removing the decaying bus station. It would also build over and pedestrianise Cannon Street, which had physically isolated the northern part of the centre, and make it easier for shoppers to walk around the shops.

Planning permissions, which of course were a necessity to enable the construction process, were secured following detailed discussions and liaisons between Prudential, their design team and Manchester City Council. By September 2003 all necessary consents were in place, and the project commenced with the demolition of the northern part of the centre. Finally, the Arndale Bus Station would be removed from the city centre, seven years after the bomb. It also led to demolition of the Cromford Court apartments, one of the first residential schemes in the city centre.

▼ Arndale Centre extension under construction.

Stephen Welsh

Over a three-year period the three phases would be delivered as follows:

One   Opened in October 2005, housing a 150,000sq ft (14,00m²) four-storey Next – the largest ever built – as well as River Island, Nike, Starbucks and Eat.

Two   A new mall, comprising a 45,000sq ft (4,180m²) Topshop and other retailers such Bershka, Monsoon and Bank.

Three   Opened in September 2006 with shops such as Waterstone's, New Look, Virgin and Sports World.

▲   Entrance to Next, Arndale Centre, on the corner of Shudehill and Corporation Street.

What is most noticeable about the revitalised centre is the diversity of the retail offer and, also, the natural flow from the western part of the city's retail core (Harvey Nichols and Heals, for example) through to the eastern part (Arndale Market and eventually leading onto the Northern Quarter). In a sense it symbolises the expansion of the retail experience in Manchester: something for everyone.

It seems appropriate to draw a close to the story of the Arndale Centre by capturing author Bill Bryson's emotions when he officially opened the revamped Arndale Centre in October 2003. In an article published by the *BBC News*, he described the Arndale Centre as 'a thousand times better'. He also paid tribute to the centre's connections with the rest of the city:

'This used to be a cold forbidding thing separate from the city centre, now it is concentrated on what is going on around it.'

SHAMBLES WEST

As a direct replacement for the much-maligned Shambles Square Market Place, the masterplan and SPG identified the opportunity for a major retail, commercial and residential building. The detailed proposals that would follow, designed by BDP, were moulded around such objectives and sought to ensure architectural compatibility with the new Marks & Spencer store, adjacent to the site.

▼   The demolition of Shambles Square and the construction of New Cathedral Street.

Stephen Welsh

▲   The demolition of Shambles Square.

© Euan Kellie

The proposals were granted planning permission by Manchester City Council at the back-end of 1997. To the relief of many, demolition of the Shambles Square Market Place started shortly after (by this time, the wheels were turning in respect of relocating the Old Wellington and Sinclair's Oyster Bar – see the 'Historic' chapter for more information). The site was clear by late 1999 and, with the turn of the millennium, work could begin on the new 'Shambles West' development. The final scheme would comprise three key elements: a new destination store, new retail units and a new residential building. In respect of the latter, in 2000 Crosby Homes, were appointed by landowners Prudential to develop a £20 million residential scheme that would follow the principles of the masterplan and act as a landmark for the scheme. This would be known as No.1 Deansgate.

These were exciting times. It was announced in 2000 that the 300,000sq ft (27,800m²) landmark store at Shambles West would be occupied by Harvey Nichols – the upmarket department store. This was big news for Manchester. It would be one of only six cities in the UK to boast such a retailer. It was a far cry from the shops that used to occupy the Shambles Square Market Place, with traders in the 1980s and 1990s such as Sussex Armoury and Ath:Leisure. The store opened its doors in August 2003.

▲ Shambles Square, 1984.

Manchester Archives and Local Studies

▼ Harvey Nichols advert, Great Ancoats Street.

© Aidan O'Rourke - www.aidan.co.uk

▲ Final work to Harvey Nichols, September 2002.

▼ Harvey Nichols, New Cathedral Street.

© Euan Kellie

© Aidan O'Rourke - www.aidan.co.uk

REBUILDING **MANCHESTER**

▶ New Cathedral Street.

As the scheme came out of the ground, more and more upmarket retailers expressed an interest in occupying space and, one by one, they were signed up. By the time the development was complete in August 2002 the units were occupied by Zara, Reiss, Hobbs, Heals and Rockport. Suddenly the shopping experience in Manchester was radically changing.

'THE TRIANGLE'

The final piece of the jigsaw was that of the refurbished Corn Exchange. Having considered several potential uses, the final scheme that was chosen by owners Frogmore Estates was a total contrast to the small independent trader experience that existed before the bomb.

It was branded 'The Triangle' (in reference to the shape of the Corn Exchange) and would comprise three floors of retail and leisure space – almost 100,000sq ft in total (9,290m^2) – targeting retailers in the same genre as Habitat. The Triangle opened in August 2000 and in the first year attracted a number of retailers, including shops from King Street such as Jigsaw, while also attracting new tenants such as Muji, Jerry's Home Store, Gant, Space NK and Bravissimo.

In 2001 Frogmore Estates went on to sell the building for £50 million to Blackstone and Milligan; it has since changed hands again. In turn, the type of retailers inside the building changed from fashion to outdoor pursuits. By 2010 a number of the units were empty. As captured by Cathy Malcolm in her video entitled *Bombed Out*, released in June

▼ 'Shopping at Exchange Square', September 2002.

▲ The Triangle, Exchange Square.

2006, Afflecks (Palace) has retained the same atmosphere and sense of independence in the years following the bomb, while the Corn Exchange has changed entirely. In a sense, it raises the question as to whether the Corn Exchange has come full circle following the bomb – maybe now is the time for small traders to take up space in the building again?

◄ Afflecks.

Independent Retailers: Individual Shops and Individual Styles

It is very important to appreciate that, while the retail core experienced great change in the years following the bomb, Manchester is not just about 'top end' expensive fashion outlets.

Indeed, one of the greatest strengths of Manchester's retail offer is that of the independents: small traders with creativity and independence, all located within walking distance of the Arndale Centre, Harvey Nichols and the Triangle. In the city centre many of these traders can be found in the Northern Quarter. Anchored by Afflecks (previously Afflecks Palace), which opened in 1981, there is a wonderful blend of retailers in this part of the city, with shops such as Retro Rehab and Pop Boutique offering vintage clothes. Similarly, the Manchester Craft and Design Centre (previously the Craft Village), which opened in 1982, has dozens of independent stalls, small shops and boutiques.

▼► Craft Centre.

▲▼ Arndale Market.

Edward Chadwick

Edward Chadwick

Edward Chadwick

Afflecks Manchester

Edward Chadwick

© Euan Kellie

© Euan Kellie

◀▼ Arndale Market.

CONCLUSION

The shopping experience in Manchester city centre has changed dramatically over the years, particularly following the bomb. It is now one of the most visited retail destinations in the UK, with a wonderful, diverse mix of shops and traders from Harvey Nichols through to the Arndale Market, then onto the Northern Quarter and the hundreds of small businesses.

Cityco, Manchester's City Centre Management Company, has played a key role in this success, working with partners such as Manchester City Council, GMPTE and Marketing Manchester to attract key retailers to the city. As a measure of success and influence, in 2009 they successfully co-ordinated a marketing campaign to promote the variety of retail and leisure facilities in Manchester, including TV, radio, press, outdoor and print material.

There are still challenges for the future, however. Former retail arteries such as King Street and St Ann's Square are no longer what they used to be, with people now choosing to shop elsewhere (reflected by shops locating in other parts of the city centre). Similarly, parts of the centre have been badly affected by the economic downturn (such as parts of Deansgate), leading to vacant units. It is this continual re-positioning within the main retail centre that will also need to be anticipated as the market perpetually adjusts itself and new retail space is created in places such as Spinningfields.

▼ Church Street Market.

▼ Piccadilly Market.

SEE WHAT MANCHESTER'S MADE OF

Manchester city centre Christmas marketing campaign 2009 (co-ordinated by Cityco, Manchester's city-entre management company).

'Manchester has a deserved reputation as a city that thinks a table is for dancing on.'

– Mark Radcliffe

LEISURE

BEFORE THE BOMB

What do we mean by leisure? In this instance it means the use of time outside of work (shopping has been covered in the 'Retail' chapter, but that is not to say for one minute that it is not sometimes a leisure experience!). The city council has endeavoured for years to make sure that there is ample leisure space available in the city centre. And why not? If the city centre was just a place to work then it would be no different to a large business park, off a motorway junction, in the middle of nowhere; devoid of soul, life and vibrancy.

In fact, leisure and recreation in Manchester has been in existence for as long as people can remember. During the Industrial Revolution, the city may have been the hub of activity and commerce, with people working all hours on the canals, railways and in the warehouses. But it was also a place where the wealthy industrialists wanted to create a city that was about more than just commerce.

Beerhouses were the first form of recreational pursuit, provided for the workers. Not a bad start. The website www.northmanchester.net contains a fascinating overview of the evolution of pubs in the centre of Manchester. Pubs that can be traced back to the years before the Industrial Revolution came in the form of the Old Wellington and Sinclair's Oyster Bar, The Crown and Cushion on Corporation Street, which was built in the early 20th century on the site of the Old Crown (opened around 1741), and the Pack Horse on Deansgate, which was built in the 1890s on the site of a century-old alehouse.

In line with the city's growth and economic success came a wider range of leisure opportunities for those with time (and money) on their hands. For those with an interest in theatre, Manchester could offer the Palace Theatre on Oxford Street (1891), the Opera House on Quay Street (1912) and more recently the Royal Exchange Theatre (1976).

REBUILDING **MANCHESTER**

In terms of museums, the city has the Museum of Science and Industry (1983) and the People's History Museum (1994, refurbished 2010). The city centre also has several art galleries: The Manchester Art Gallery on Mosley Street (1825, extended 2002), The Cornerhouse on Oxford Road (a former carpet shop, reopened in 1985), the Athenaeum and the Cube Gallery on Portland Street (1998).

For those with an interest in reading, there is no shortage of libraries. In 1850 Manchester had been the first local authority in Britain to introduce a public lending and reference library. Lending of books was free, with the costs being supported by ratepayers. Chetham's Library, part of the School of Music, opened in 1653 and is still open to the public today. It is also the oldest free public reference library in the United Kingdom. Indeed, it was a favoured meeting location for Engels and Marx during the frequent visits to the city. There is also the Central Library in St Peter's Square.

▼ Central Library.

◄ John Ryland's Library, Deansgate.

The building was designed by London architect E. Vincent Harris, and it was officially opened by King George on 17 July 1934. Furthermore, the city has the John Rylands Library and The Portico Library on Mosley Street (completed in 1806).

It is hard to know where to start when commenting on Manchester's musical heritage, but it is probably best to start off with classical music and opera. The Halle Orchestra, which is the oldest professional orchestra in Britain and was founded by Charles Halle, first played at the Free Trade Hall in 1858. It remained their home until 1996 when they relocated to the Bridgewater Hall. The Manchester Camerata was founded in 1972 and is also based at the Bridgewater Hall. There is the wonderful BBC Philharmonic Orchestra which has, over the years, had several concert venues in Manchester: Houldsworth Hall, the Town Hall and for many years the Free Trade Hall.

The modern music industry has much to thank Manchester for. In terms of bands and contributors the list is huge: Oasis, Happy Mondays, Joy Division, Stone Roses and New Order, to offer a quick sample. It seems appropriate at this point to acknowledge the legendary Anthony H. Wilson and Factory Records – a story captured entertainingly by the 2002 film, *24 Hour Party People*. Allied with this, some of the earliest examples of nightclubs included The Ritz on Whitworth Street (1927) and more recently, of course, the Hacienda (1982) on Whitworth Street West and Sankeys Soap at the converted Beehive Mill off Great Ancoats Street (1994).

REBUILDING **MANCHESTER**

▶ Chinese Arch, China Town.

▼ Hong Kong restaurant, China Town.

DISTINCT LOCALITIES

In tandem with the expansion of Manchester city centre, a number of distinct localities have emerged. The boundaries of these areas are fluid, reflected by the activities, functions, and sense of place around the margins of each area. In a sense, they reflect the interplay between the themes introduced in the book: the link between people living and working in an area, in turn creating leisure destinations as bars and shops begin to appear.

The first of these is **China Town**, which is focused around Faulkner Street and in close proximity to Mosley Street and the central business district. The Chinese community started to arrive in Manchester around the 1940s, with the first Chinese restaurant in the city centre, the Ping Hong on Mosley Street, opening in 1948. The area gradually expanded as the vacant cotton warehouses around Nicholas Street, Faulkner Street and George Street were converted to Chinese restaurants such as Charlie Chan's (1973), the Woo Sang (1976) and the Little Yang Sing (1978). Piece by piece, a distinct, compact community began to appear and became home to many restaurants, shops and small businesses, as well as significant levels of housing (reflected by some of the residential schemes listed in the 'Residential' chapter).

During a similar time period, Manchester's **Gay Village**, centred around Chorlton Street and Canal Street, and just a few minutes' walk from Piccadilly Gardens, appeared on the scene. Anchored around Sackville Street, Whitworth Street and Princess Street, it began with a series of venues: The New Union, Napoleans and the Rembrant, all located on Canal Street. As it grew in popularity, 'The Village', as it is more commonly known, began to emerge from the shadows, marked by the opening of the bar 'Manto' by pioneering property developer Carol Ainscow and business partner Peter Dalton in 1991. Like many of the stories told in this book, the bar captured the entrepreneurial spirit of Manchester by doing things differently and with confidence. Rather than hiding its light under a bushel, the bar burst out onto Canal Street by using a plate glass window and, later, balconies and pavement tables. Manto was a success. More gay and lesbian clubs and bars followed in the city centre shortly after, with additions such as Cruz 101 (1992) and Paradise Factory (1994).

The **Northern Quarter** also emerged as a proudly independent part of the city during this period. As touched on in the 'Retail' chapter, the area historically was the centre of the city's market activity in Smithfield and, for many years, the retail hub of the centre. In perhaps an ironic twist, it was the realignment of the retail core, assisted predominantly by the Arndale Centre in the 1970s, that led to the direct availability of cheap, vacant warehouse, office and retail space in this part of the city centre. This provided opportunities for new businesses, wholesale fashion traders and the cultural industries.

During the 1980s and 1990s the diversity of the local businesses and occupiers continued with the opening of bars such as Dry Bar on Oldham Street, which was opened in 1989 by the successful Manchester band New Order, along with cauldrons of creativity such as Afflecks in 1981 and the Manchester Craft Village in 1982.

Finally, **Castlefield**, which before the bomb had become the home of creative industries (outlined in more detail in 'Welcome to Manchester' and the 'Residential' chapters). The opening of the bar and restaurant known as Dukes 92 in 1991 (named because of its position next to the 92nd and final lock on the Rochdale Canal – see 'Space and Connectivity' for more) and the Atlas bar at 376 Deansgate in 1994, designed by Simpson Associates, was symbolic of the culture that was emerging in Manchester at the time; a creative European city with loft apartments, converted mills and warehouses, cafés and bars serving lattes and espressos and diverse and mixed communities with a range of leisure and cultural attractions.

AFTER THE BOMB

So by the time of the bomb on 15 June 1996, Manchester had already managed to position itself as a city with much to offer. In terms of 'what happened next', three distinct layers have emerged.

▲ Queer, Canal Street.

▲ Manto, Canal Street.

▲ The Rembrandt, Canal Street.

▲ Dry Bar, Oldham Street.

REBUILDING **MANCHESTER**

▲ Atlas, Deansgate.

▲ Barca, Catalan Square, Castlefield.

EXPANSION OF EXISTING QUARTERS

Firstly, in the years that have followed the bomb, Manchester's distinct quarters have strengthened and grown. Canal Street and The Village has continued to attract investment from noteworthy individuals such as Take That manager Nigel Martin-Smith, who invested in bars such as Essential and Queer, along with other local investors who delivered venues such as Taurus, Vanilla, Thompson's and Hollywood. The community spirit has evolved to the point where there are now Village taxis, barbers and doctors. The evolution of the Village has not been without its problems, and in some cases it has become a victim of its own success: the 'Origin' proposal on Whitworth Street and Princess Street is an excellent case in point (see 'Residential' chapter for futher detail).

Castlefield has seen mixed success. Some of the bars that were opened in the mid-to-late 1990s have suffered, perhaps due to Castlefield's fragmented geographic location compared to other parts of the city centre. In 1996, on the back of Dukes 92, Barca bar was completed, located in the heart of the Castlefield Basin. It was a joint venture between Hale Leisure and So What Arts (who managed Simply Red). It is understood that the name Barca was selected by Simply Red singer, Mick Hucknall, to evoke the sophisticated bar culture of a great European city – Barcelona. After years of trading, the bar closed in 2008 but reopened a year later.

In 1998 The Quay Bar, developed by Wolverhampton and Dudley Breweries and designed by architects Stephenson Bell, opened in Castlefield, located on the edge of the Bridgewater Canal. The objective at the time was to provide a contemporary solution that offered both living space for the bar manager along with dining and bar space.

▶ Quay Bar, Castlefield, 1998.

204

Andy Davison

▲ The derelict Quay Bar.

▲ Quay Bar, Chester Road.

▼ Inside Quay Bar.

The wonderful, elegant design made it very different to the other recent buildings and conversions in the Castlefield Basin, all of which were red-brick Victorian structures. In recognition of its architectural quality the bar was shortlisted in 1999 for the Stirling Prize UK Building of the Year. Unfortunately, in the years that followed the turn of the millennium it is understood the bar struggled financially and closed in 2003. Developers Urban Splash acquired the unit and, for a brief period, it was reopened and rebranded as the Modo Clubroom.

Sadly, the building was closed again in 2005 and, following several arson attacks, was subsequently demolished in 2007. This, without question, was a major disappointment for architect Roger Stephenson, captured by an interview with the *Architects Journal*, published on 22 November 2007:

'The battle to deliver the building took a few years off my life, and it was the only bar to ever reach the Stirling Prize shortlist, so it's doubly upsetting to see it ripped apart.'

By late 2010 the site previously occupied by the building was still vacant.

▶ Vacant Quay Bar site, February 2010.

© Euan Kellie

Iclan Developments

▲ Bluu Bar, Smithfield.

A third bar and restaurant, Jackson's Wharf, opened in 1998 and, much like Quay Bar, traded for less than a decade. By 2004 it was closed and as outlined in the 'Residential' chapter, despite proposals for redevelopment, the site at the beginning of 2010 was marked by the vacant building.

It has not all been doom and gloom, though. Other parts of Castlefield have been successful, helped by the completion of the Urban Splash developments Timber Wharf, Modo and The Boxworks. In alliance with these schemes, bars, shops and restaurants have begun to appear, thereby supporting the expanding community and providing a destination for visitors. Other notable additions in Castlefield include Alberts Shed on Castle Street, adjacent to Dukes 92.

The Northern Quarter has experienced sustained success and growth. In the years that have followed the bomb many new attractions have appeared. This has included pubs and bars: Bluu Bar on High Street (part of the Smithfield development), TV21 on Thomas Street, The Northern on Oldham Street and Lammars off Newton Street (Pride Of Manchester Awards winner of Best Bar 2008–09); art galleries: The Richard Goodall Gallery on Thomas Street and The Art Surgery on Tib Street; cafés and restaurants: Café Pop, Centro, The Soup Kitchen and Drip Coffee; music venues: Night and Day Café and Matt and Phreds Jazz Club; and a host of small businesses, many in the so-called 'creative industries'.

▼ Chinese New Year, China Town.

© Cityco (Manchester's City Centre Management Company)

Similarly China Town has continued to grow in significance. Manchester's Chinese community is now the second largest in Europe, and the spectacular Chinese New Year celebrations are one of the fastest growing visitor attractions in the city's events calendar, attracting over 55,000 people each year. The area is now home to over 30 restaurants, Oriental supermarkets, Chinese medicine shops and casinos.

NEW ENTERTAINMENT VENUES

The second major trend has been the completion of new, landmark entertainment venues and complexes across the city centre, varying in size and scale but all playing a major role in attracting visitors into the city centre during the day and evening, seven days a week.

MANCHESTER EVENING NEWS ARENA

A year before the bomb, one of the most important new buildings in the city centre was completed: the Nynex Arena (now known as the Manchester Evening News Arena). Located behind Victoria Station, the arena was originally part of Manchester's 2000 Olympic Games bid (see 'Welcome to Manchester'). Designed by DLA Architecture, it officially opened on Saturday 15 July 1995 when Torvill & Dean, British ice dancers and former British, European, Olympic and World champions, broke the UK box office attendance record for a single ice performance, watched by over 15,000 people inside the venue. It important also to recognise the size of the venue: the capacity of 21,000 made it, at the time of completion, the largest indoor arena in Europe.

▲   Manchester Evening News Arena.

In the years that have followed it has become one of the most important destinations in Manchester city centre and one of the busiest venues in the world. It attracts over one million visitors a year and was voted the 'International Venue of the Year' by industry publication Pollstar in 2002. The success of the arena is undoubtedly due to its flexibility. In terms of live music performances, the list is first class: U2, The Rolling Stones, Madonna and Pavarotti. Indeed, Bono of U2 was so satisfied that, according to the arena website, he described it in 2002 as 'the best concert venue in the country'.

It has also been home to the Manchester Storm and Manchester Phoenix ice hockey teams, and the Manchester Giants basketball team. Boxers Ricky Hatton, Joe Calzaghe, Mike Tyson, Jeff Lacy, Kostya Tszyu and other world champions have fought at the arena, and the World Wrestling Entertainment has hosted multiple events over the years.

THE PRINTWORKS

Manchester City Council's SPG for the bomb-damaged area identified that the area bound by Shudehill, Withy Grove, Corporation Street and Miller Street had:

'...potential to provide a major leisure complex of regional status which whilst being a major visitor attraction in its own right will also complement surrounding economic activity and be a significant addition to the facilities of the Regional Core.'

This was not the first time the area had been identified for a major development. In June 1992 the city council had granted Shudehill Developments Limited planning permission for a major development which comprised a shopping centre, residential apartments, craft workshops and civic spaces. Despite the council's endorsement, like other major proposals at the time the scheme had not been built.

Following the international urban design competition, it was recognised by West Midlands-based developer twins Don and Roy Richardson (known as Richardson Developments) that a major new leisure destination would work extremely well in this part of the city centre. The site in question was made up of temporary car parks, untidy scrub land and dominated by one building: Thompson House, the old printing works of The Mirror Group. The building had been vacant since 1987 and had a dominant façade on the corner of Corporation Street and Withy Grove.

▶ The Printworks under construction

Stephen Welsh

▲ Demolition of Thompson House for The Printworks development.

Stephen Welsh

▲▼ The Printworks under construction.

Stephen Welsh

▶ The Printworks.

Richardson Developments and their design team entered discussions with Manchester Millennium and the city council. It was concluded that a scheme could be delivered on the site that would work commercially while also retaining the façade of Thompson House (the rear of the building would be demolished). In September 1997 two planning applications were submitted to Manchester City Council. The vision was to deliver a new retail and leisure destination known as 'The Printworks' (recognition of the use of the building as a Printworks and its historic importance to Manchester). The scheme would comprise 495,000sq ft (46,000m^2) of space with a mix of entertainment, leisure, retail and restaurant uses. It was approved by the city council, within two months, with permission granted on 7 November 1997.

During determination of the application Richardson's secured a number of leisure operators for the scheme, including United Cinemas International (UCI) in late 1997 who would act as an anchor with a 20-screen multiplex cinema. A year

Stephen Welsh

◄ Cathedral Gardens site before redevelopment.

later, and as a sign of confidence in the scheme and its location, Hard Rock Café chose the Printworks to be the location for, at the time, only its third UK outlet. The new bar-cum-club operator, Tiger Tiger, which had opened its first unit in London's Haymarket in 1998, also chose to locate within the Printworks.

As with all elements of the bomb rebuilding, development was prompt. The site was cleared through much of 1998, and by 1999 the development began to appear behind the façade of Thompson House. The Printworks opened in November 2000, with Lionel Ritchie performing live outside the venue to thousands of people. The final line-up was impressive: a 20-screen UCI multiplex, an IMAX cinema, a Holmes Place health and fitness centre, and a number of bars and restaurants, including Hard Rock Café.

By 2010 the Printworks was still one of the largest leisure complexes in Europe, with figures suggesting that over nine million people visit the complex each year.

URBIS

The vision for the Urbis (latin for 'of the city') was included within the Edaw masterplan and guidance for the bomb-damaged area. The site, at the time of the bomb, was in use as a car park located within the Millennium Quarter and represented a clear development opportunity. It also had strong historic connections; it was land that Frederick Engels knew as 'Little Gibraltar', at the time a collage of run-down housing and grimy courts, captured in his book *The Condition of the Working Class in England.*

▲ Urbis, under construction.

▲ 'See your world differently' – Urbis, opening 27 June 2002.

REBUILDING **MANCHESTER**

Andrea Ku

▲ Urbis, Corporation Street.

▼ Urbis and Millennium Quarter.

An international design competition was held for the site, won by Ian Simpson Architects. The concept was to deliver a seven-storey building clad entirely in glass which would act as a visitor centre and a worthy landmark for this new piece of the city centre. As outlined by the city council's Planning Committee Report on 28 October 1999, the drive was to deliver a scheme which 'focused on the experience of the "modern city"'. It would also sit within the 'City Park' (later known as Cathedral Gardens).

The importance of partnerships in the delivery of Urbis is outlined in the book *Manchester: Shaping the City*:

'The success of the project is a result of the close working partnerships that have developed between the architect and the client, through the evolution and interpretation of the brief.'

The building opened in June 2002 and has gone on to include excellent exhibitions including the 'Peter Saville Show' in 2004, featuring the work of Manchester's famous graphic designer. The plans for the future of the building as the home of the 'Museum of Football' are certainly exciting. In an article published by *Manchester Evening News* on 8 September 2009, City Council Leader Sir Richard Leese outlined the vision:

'Manchester is renowned around the world for its footballing heritage and attracts more visitors than any English city outside London. Having a nationally significant football destination here would make perfect sense so when the National Football Museum approached us we were naturally keen to explore this exciting idea. Talks have been very positive so far.'

© Aidan O'Rourke - www.aidan.co.uk

GREAT NORTHERN WAREHOUSE

The Great Northern Warehouse, located at the junction of Deansgate and Peter Street, has been a landmark building in the city centre since it was completed in 1899. The warehouse was located close to the Manchester Central railway station (now Manchester Central, previously GMEX), and was used to store goods that were transported via the railway. The warehouse was built above the Manchester and Salford Junction Canal, and a dock beneath the building was constructed to allow goods to be transferred to and from canal barges.

Following its closure in 1963 as part of the infamous Beeching Report (introduced in 'Welcome to Manchester') the building lay vacant (the city council recognised its historic value and sought to protect the building. On 4 May 1979 it was designated a Grade II* listing). Over the 20 years that followed, the site was time and time again the subject of various development proposals, but nothing

Stephen Welsh

◀ Buildings on Peter Street, cleared as part of Great Northern Warehouse development.

came to fruition. The only appropriate use that could be found at this time was as a temporary multi-storey car park . In 1994, at the invitation of the city council, English Partnerships agreed to lead an analysis of regeneration potential for the wider GMEX area centred around the Great Northern Warehouse.

A masterplan was subsequently prepared in 1995 and endorsed by several parties, including the city council. A key element of the plan was the conversion of the Great Northern Warehouse for leisure and retail uses. There were three key phases: Phases 1 and 2 were developed for retail and leisure (including an AMC cinema), while Phase 3 was to be a 345-bed Hilton Hotel (now Beetham Tower – covered in the 'Residential' chapter). Planning permission was granted by the city council in March 1996. Developers Morrison Merlin could finally commence the £100 million metamorphosis of the Warehouse.

Work began in 1998 with the clearance of buildings along Peter Street (within the Peter Street conservation area) and demolition of the listed viaduct

© Aidan O'Rourke - www.aidan.co.uk

▲ Outside the Great Northern Warehouse before redevelopment, 1997.

▼ Windmill Street looking towards Great Northern Warehouse.

Stephen Welsh

▼ The Great Northern Warehouse and viaduct in 1996.

Stephen Welsh

▼ 'Get Up 'N' Go', Great Northern Warehouse advert, April 2002.

© Euan Kellie

▼ Demolition of the Great Northern Warehouse viaduct.

Stephen Welsh

▲   Manchester 235, Watson Street.

along Deansgate and Great Bridgewater Street. Prior to the clearance, the Warehouse, and the space fronting onto Peter Street, was in use as a car park.

The revamped Warehouse and cinema opened in 2001. In the decade that followed, the scheme has not quite worked as a true leisure destination in the city centre (reflected perhaps by the number of times it has changed ownership; from Morrison Construction to AWG in 2000; from AWG to Capital and Regional in 2005). New attractions have, however, been introduced, most notably the casino 'Manchester 235' on Watson Street which opened in October 2006. The website captures the ethos:

'Manchester 235 is affordable luxury for everyone. Built across two floors of dramatic design, Manchester 235 is all about Las Vegas-style glamour and excitement and is quite unlike anything else Manchester has to offer.'

In early 2009 Manchester City Council looked to acquire the building – the talks, however, came to nothing. With the right blend of uses there can be little doubt that one day the project will become an established leisure destination in Manchester city centre.

DEANSGATE LOCKS

Elsewhere in the city centre plans were afoot in the late 1990s to create what would, in years to come, become a new leisure destination in its own right: Deansgate Locks.

The proposals put forward to the city council by developers Westport sought to reuse 12 railway arches along Whitworth Street West, adjacent to the Bridgewater Canal, and in close proximity to the former Hacienda nightclub and Castlefield. While relatively small in terms of floorspace (only 55,000sq ft or 5,110m^2), the development would include a number of bars, designed by various architects including Raw Design (Loaf) and Ian Simpson Architects (Baa Bar). The city council supported the vision, and planning permission was granted 18 September 1997.

By late 1999, as construction was underway at the Locks, developers Westport secured a tenant of real note: The Comedy Store. Established in London in 1979, the Store attracted some of the first alternative comedians, now household names: Rik Mayall, Adrian Edmondson, Alexei Sayle, Jennifer Saunders, Dawn French, Keith Allen, Peter Richardson, Nigel Planer and Arnold Brown, to name but a few. Now it would finally, after a five-year search, have a

▲   Deansgate Locks.

▶   Deansgate Locks under refurbishment, 1999.

© Aidan O'Rourke - www.aidan.co.uk

sister venue. Owner of the Comedy Store, Don Ward, expressed his delight in an article published by the *Estates Gazette* on 1 October 1999:

'After 20 years in London, I could think of no better way to celebrate than to open a second Comedy Store in Manchester.'

Sporting a 500-seat auditorium, along with a bar and diner, the new Comedy Store at Deansgate Locks opened on 14 September 2000, with proceedings led by comedians Paul Merton and Julian Clary.

HOTELS AND TOURISM

A symbol of Manchester's success has been that of the rapidly expanding hotel market and the tourist industry.

HOTELS

Back in 1984 there were only five hotels operating in the city centre: The Midland, The Britannia, The Grand, Hotel Piccadilly at Piccadilly Plaza and the Portland Thistle Hotel – providing a total of 1,287 bedrooms. The city council's assessment of the hotel market, published in 1985, concluded that it was unlikely the market would grow due to the lack of business and visitors at the weekend. This was not helped by the fact that the majority of tourist attractions, which at the time included the Air and Space Museum at the Museum of Science and Industry, were mostly day facilities.

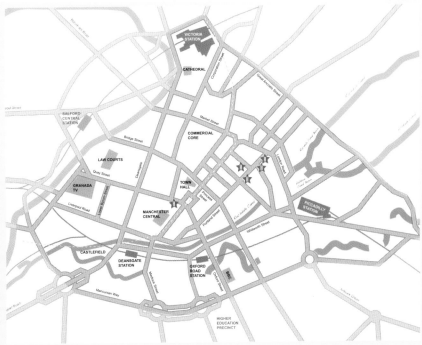

▲ Hotels in the city centre, 1984.

In the 25 years that have followed, the city centre has experienced significant growth across a host of sectors. This has, in turn, led to increased demand for the city centre as a place for hotel accommodation. Between 1998 and 2002 the supply of hotel bedrooms almost doubled, increasing from 2,527 to 4,167, and between 2001 and 2005, Manchester's hotel occupancy rates were consistently above average rates for the UK (in 2001 the occupancy rate for the UK was 69.7 per cent and Manchester 71.1 per cent; in 2005 the rates were 71.9 per cent and 75 per cent respectively). The supply of hotel bedspaces continued to increase rapidly in the period from early 2003 through to 2008 when it was estimated that there were 6,393 bedroom spaces in the city centre, comprising 34 graded hotels. An increase of 500 per cent from 1985.

What has also been interesting is the blend of hotel types that have appeared in Manchester city centre, particularly during the first decade of the new millennium. This has included new buildings, innovative refurbishments and conversions, providing visitors a choice from the 'top-end' five-star offer through to the three-star budget offer. According to MIDAS (Manchester Investment Development Agency Service), by 2009 there were 428 five-star hotel bedrooms, 2,734 four-star and 3,231 three-star.

Some of the most notable new hotel schemes have included:

- The opening of the 263-bedroom Radisson Edwardian Hotel at the Free Trade Hall in late 2004 – the city's only five-star hotel at the time. This was not a simple project – see 'Historic' chapter for more information.

- A series of hotels completed on the fringe of the city centre in 2005, including the former Le Meridien which was converted to the Marriott Victoria & Albert Hotel, providing 158 bedrooms and the Travelodge on Great Ancoats Street.

- The completion of 'luxury' hotels in 2006 including The Hilton, as part of Beetham Tower; the City Inn, as part of the Piccadilly Place scheme, and the Macdonald Hotel by Piccadilly Station.

- The 303-bedroom Midland Hotel was acquired by Quintessential Hotels for £36 million and underwent a £15 million refurbishment programme, completed in 2007.

- The trend continued with the completion of the Crowne Plaza on Shudehill (part of the Smithfield Ician development) in 2008, representing the continued expansion of the city centre.

- By 2010 further hotels were in the 'pipeline', including the W Hotel as part of the 'Origin' development and the Pillo Hotel, designed by architects HKR, on Whitworth Street West.

Jonathan Langston, Managing Director of TRI Hospitality Consulting, captures the importance and relevance of hotels:

'Branded hotels are often viewed as being a significant feature in the development of a destination. The existence of such product gives travellers the confidence of a minimum standard of product and service, with which they will often have familiarity, and sets the tone of the experience. It can convey a sentiment that a market has matured to a sufficient extent that a branded hotel of significant scale, range and standard of facilities is supportable, which endorses the destination as a place in which to do business or spend leisure time.'

◄ Hotels in Manchester city centre, 2009.

TOURISM

In alliance with the growth of hotels, the number of people visiting Greater Manchester and Manchester city centre also increased dramatically in the first decade of the millennium due to a host of factors, including the leisure and retail offer, a growing conference sector (directly related to the business growth outlined in the 'Commercial' chapter), sustained demand for business travellers and the 2002 Commonwealth Games. The latter, in particular, played a major role in raising the profile of the city centre both in the UK and overseas.

According to Cityco data, the figures are certainly compelling:

• Between 1999 and 2004, the number of visitors to Greater Manchester increased from 77.1 million to 90.7 million – a rise of 17.6 per cent.

• The value of tourism to Greater Manchester increased from £3.05 billion in 2000 to £5.6 billion in 2007.

• Overnight stays in Manchester city reached 971,000 in 2007 – a significant increase from 770,000 in 2004 and 260,000 in 2000.

• In 2009 Manchester had the third-highest (after Edinburgh and London) tourist spending in the UK by overseas residents (totalling £405 million per annum).

• In 2009 Manchester was voted the third-best conference destination in the world following a poll conducted by Conference and Incentive Travel. It was beaten only by London and Barcelona.

© The Neighbourhood

▶ Visualisation of Pillo Hotel, Whitworth Street West.

REBUILDING **MANCHESTER**

▲ Great Manchester Run.

▲ Glasgow Rangers fans in Piccadilly Gardens,
14 May 2008.

▼ Usain Bolt sprinting down Deansgate, 17 May
2009.

STAGE FOR MAJOR EVENTS

The final strand to the story is perhaps the most important – using the expanded city centre as an arena for innovative local, national and international events. This is made possible by committed individuals, businesses and organisations, organised and facilitated by the city council.

From politics to pride and Brown to Bolt, the city centre has truly become a stage for a diverse range of activities. The awards that the city has scooped are equally wide ranging, including Best 'Sports City' in the world in 2008 (beating Melbourne, Berlin, New York and Moscow in the process).

Genre	Events
Music	Manchester International Festival, DPercussion, Manchester Jazz Festival, In The City.
Sporting	FINA World Swimming Championships 2008, BUPA Great City Games, Great Manchester Run, Commonwealth Games 2002, Euro '96, UEFA Cup Final 2008.
Political	Labour and Conservative Party Conferences.
Food and Drink	Specialist Markets (including the European Christmas Markets), Manchester Food & Drink Festival.
Civic	Manchester Pride, Manchester Day, Manchester Irish Festival, Chinese New Year celebrations.

CONCLUSION

Four years after the bomb, an article published by *The Independent* on 10 September 2000 summarised Manchester's progress:

'Stylistically, Manchester is still head and shoulders above the rest of the country. The city that gave birth to the style bar and kicked off Britain's club scene also initiated the country's adventure with post-industrial design; to use the old for the new. Around the town centre, ultra-modern clubs, galleries and bars peek out from the basements of grand Victorian monoliths.'

This statement is without question still valid in 2010. Manchester city centre is a place where people come together, a place of vibrancy, diversity, creativity and activity, a place many people want and choose to visit – it is the city's playground! The 'Manchester Day' parade, to be held for the first time on 20 June 2010, captures this spirit. It is introduced on the official website as a 'unique and original celebration based on all the things we love about this great city, the dreams it inspires and the ideas it brings to life.'

As the city centre continues to change and grow, this continued creativity will strengthen Manchester as a local, regional, national and international destination.

'Manchester has everything except a beach.'

– Ian Brown

SPACE AND CONNECTIVITY

BEFORE THE BOMB

Time for the final strand of the story: the pedestrian experience in Manchester city centre. There are many ways in which this can be assessed. For some it is gauged by the quality and quantity of public open space; for others it is the ability to walk from destination A to B; it can also be dictated by first impressions when arriving into the city by car or rail. This chapter will try to take into account all of these characteristics, but first some background.

In terms of dedicated public open space, some of the first pieces in Manchester city centre were provided at the tail-end of the 19th century and early 20th century; in most cases a direct response to the falling city-centre population and, in turn, parishioners. In chronological order; at the northern end of the city (off Deansgate) St Mary's Church and Yard, which had been constructed in the 1756, suffered from a declining congregation in the late 19th century. Consequently it was acquired by the Manchester Corporation (now Manchester City Council) and demolished in 1891. This became Parsonage Gardens (much of which has remained unchanged since this time).

To the rear of the Town Hall is St Peter's Square, previously home to St Peter's Church which was designed by architect James Wyatt and built between 1788 and 1794. The area historically consisted of fields on, at the time, the outskirts of the small Georgian town of Manchester. Famously, it was near the location of the Peterloo Massacre in 1831 (a site occupied by the converted Free Trade Hall). By the beginning of the 20th century the area had become increasingly commercial (marked by the completion of the Midland Hotel in 1903) and, consequently, the church was demolished in 1907. A cenotaph designed by the architect Sir Edwin Lutyens was erected on the site in 1924.

Finally, St John's Gardens in Castlefield. The site had previously been occupied by St John's Church, completed in 1768. In 1930 the Ecclesiastical Commission handed the building and the site over to Manchester City Council, which was

▼ St Peter's Church, 1907.

Royal Infirmary, Piccadilly, 1905.

Sackville Gardens.

subsequently demolished in 1931 and replaced with St John's Gardens. Two of the stained-glass windows from the church were transferred to St Ann's Church in St Ann's Square, while a monument to the church and the 22,000 people buried in its grounds stands in the middle of the gardens where the entrance to the church once lay. Some notable people were buried in the grounds of the church, including William Marsden, who in the 1840s had successfully campaigned for an early finish for workers on Saturdays (a landmark employment case). Also buried there is John Owens, founder of Owens College in 1851 which was the first college of the Victoria University of Manchester – now known as the University of Manchester.

Two further spaces were created by the city council during this time period, the first of which was Piccadilly Gardens. From 1755 the site was occupied by the Manchester Royal Infirmary until it vacated the building and moved to Oxford Road in 1910. Shortly after, the building was demolished, and by 1914 the site was clear. It went on to become the largest area of recreational open space in the city centre.

The second area of space, Sackville Gardens, is located alongside Sheena Simon College's University Science Buildings and adjacent to the Rochdale canal and opposite Canal Street. Much smaller than Piccadilly Gardens, the space was purchased by the city council in 1900 and has a somewhat formal, structured layout with amenity grassland, trees, herbaceous bedding areas and structural flowerbed planting.

After the war, many cities across the UK were left with little choice but to clear away bomb-damaged land and buildings. In turn, it was an unprecedented opportunity to remove much of the high-density Victorian built stock, the sense of congestion and the absence of public green space. The approach advocated by the 1945 City of Manchester Plan was no different:

'During the Industrial Revolution wide expanses of open land were devoured in an effort to house the rapidly growing population. Houses were built at excessive densities, without gardens, and in many cases without even backyards. Woods were destroyed, fields swallowed up, and rivers and streams turned into open sewers by a tremendous wave of "development", which, in the name of progress, obliterated all green and living things within the ever growing city.'

Author Roland Nicholas was certainly unhappy with the provision of public open space in the city centre:

'The centre of Manchester was developed largely at a time when the pursuit of commercial profit was given a free rein, and land was considered far too valuable to be wasted on parks and gardens. In consequence there is hardly any open space apart from the gardens of St. Mary's Parsonage and Piccadilly.'

According to Nicholas, only 5.5 of the 240 acres of the city centre (less than two per cent) were devoted to what he described as 'amenity purposes'.

SPACE AND CONNECTIVITY

The Plan consequently sought to remould and remodel Manchester by breaking up what Nicholas referred to as the 'amorphous mass' of the city. Many of the buildings would be replaced with more small-scale structures, anchored by parks, gardens and parades. In total 36.75 acres of public open space was to be introduced, along with a ceremonial approach from to Albert Square to Deansgate, entitled the 'processional way'.

As the city centre was rebuilt following World War Two, the protection and enhancement of space and buildings steadily became a priority. In line with the 1967 Civic Amenities Act, Manchester City Council began to introduce conservation areas across the city centre, thus providing a mechanism which would allow the council to protect or enhance sensitive parts of the city. The value attached to the quality of space and the pedestrian experience was recognised in 1968 when, as a gift, the *Manchester Evening News* paid for 28 London Plane Trees to be planted in Albert Square. The city council was delighted. In their 1969 Annual Report tributes were paid to the trees, which 'greatly enhanced the appearance and attraction of Albert Square'.

As the years rolled by, it was becoming clear that people were making decisions in terms of where to visit, live and spend money based upon the quality of a city centre – it had to be a pleasant experience. In line with this the city council continued to recognise that there was an urgent need to enhance the pedestrian experience in Manchester, particularly

▲ Lincoln Square, Brazennose Street.

▼ 'Commercial Chambers', with the Corn Exchange to the right, 1958.

▲ Outside the Corn Exchange, 1995.

▼ Market Street before pedestrianisation.

with the struggling retail market. Castlefield had made wonderful progress (it had the honour of becoming Britain's first Urban Heritage Park in 1982), and the city council had successfully created 'Lincoln Square' with the pedestrianisation of Brazennose Street. This was named after the statue of Abraham Lincoln in the centre of the square (relocated from Platt Fields in 1986) and would finally complete the 'processional way' from Albert Square through to Deansgate and on to the Law Courts as envisaged in the 1945 plan.

Notwithstanding, the city council, in the 1984 City Centre Plan, recognised that the challenge had just begun:

'In the core of the City Centre, there is however, unlikely to be any opportunity to create additional large areas of open space and the Plan therefore seeks to make the best use of the space already available. The general open space and amenity value of the Civic Squares, especially St. Ann's Square, St. Peter's Square and Albert Square, could be improved and the network of pedestrian routes between the Squares and other areas of open space could be further developed.'

Sure, there was not much land available, but in line with the council's ethos of making the best use of existing assets, progress could still be made. To achieve the greater good there would have to be sacrifices.

In February 1986 a planning application was prepared and submitted by the city council which sought approval to prepare an area of landscaped open space outside the Corn Exchange by Hanging Ditch (an area that would, in years to follow, become Exchange Square). The proposals would introduce flower beds, pedestrianised space and a fountain which would be relocated from Heaton Park – one of the biggest municipal parks in Europe. To achieve the vision it would, however, be necessary to demolish a four-storey building in the middle of the site, known as 'Commercial Chambers' (Manchester's version of the 'flat iron' building in New York). By March 1986 planning permission had been granted, the building was demolished, and the landscaped area was delivered. In October 1989, to mark the 200th anniversary of the French Revolution, the city council liaised with the French Cultural Attaché to oversee the installation of two walnut trees and a commemorative plaque placed on a cast-metal drum base. The work was paid for by the French Government. Sadly, all the trees and plaque were damaged and removed after the 1996 bomb.

By the early 1990s the city council had made real progress in terms of enhancing the pedestrian experience. Key routes and civic spaces in the city centre had been pedestrianised and/or upgraded – most notably Market Street, Albert Square, King Street and St Ann's Square. Like the fountains introduced outside the Corn Exchange, further public art was added to the city-centre street scene, including the fated obelisk at the top of Market Street (eventually removed in 1997 following concerns that it was attracting ne'er do wells).

By 15 June 1996 there was, however, still considerable work to be done, in particular the links between the two key railway stations (Piccadilly and Victoria) and the heart of the city centre; in some cases the aesthetic treatment of landmark buildings; and the enhancement of 'no go' areas.

AFTER THE BOMB

At the heart of Edaw's masterplan was the improvement of space and connectivity within the city. This was mirrored by the city council's guidance for the bomb-damaged area:

'Linkages between the rebuilt core, the rest of the Regional Centre and the surrounding regeneration areas such as the Northern Quarter and onwards to Miles Platting and Ancoats, to the existing retail and financial core, Piccadilly Gardens and the Piccadilly Station area are important and must not be overlooked.'

▲ Obelisk, Market Street, 1997.

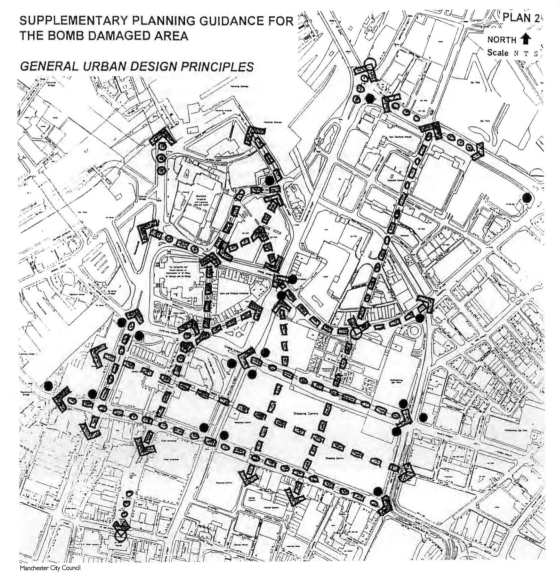

SUPPLEMENTARY PLANNING GUIDANCE FOR THE BOMB DAMAGED AREA

GENERAL URBAN DESIGN PRINCIPLES

PLAN 2

NORTH ⬆
Scale N T S

Manchester City Council

◀ General urban design principles, taken from the Manchester City Council SPG for the bomb-damaged area.

REBUILDING **MANCHESTER**

▶ The treacherous pedestrian experience along Corporation Street before the bomb.

▼ The view from St Ann's Square before New Cathedral Street.

▼ Proposed New Cathedral Street.

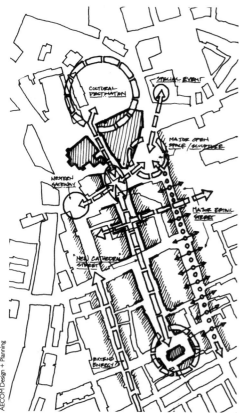

AECOM Design + Planning

Warren Marshall

It was a view shared by the public. During the design competition a public exhibition was held at the Town Hall between 25 and 27 October 1996. Three thousand people attended and viewed the models and panels that presented the short-listed masterplan entries. Over 1,000 questionnaires were completed by attendees; matters that appeared frequently included improving the external appearance of buildings, introducing more green space, and ensuring people could easily and safely walk around the city centre.

In the years that followed, the pedestrian experience in Manchester city centre was considerably enhanced. This included improved ease of movement through the city on foot, provision of high-quality public open space, upgraded transport interchanges and aesthetic improvements to some well-known 'problem' buildings.

EASE OF MOVEMENT AND 'ACTIVE FRONTAGES'

Prior to the bomb, the ability to walk around the heart of the city centre easily and safely was weak. The likelihood of someone walking from Victoria Station at the northern end of the city along Corporation Street, onto Deansgate and down to Castlefield at the southern end was limited to say the least, due mainly to the presence of obstructive blocks of development such as Shambles Square and the blank Arndale Centre frontages. There was little reason to do so, and the route was not obvious. It was also not helped by the lack of pedestrian activity and concealed streets, where the fear of criminal activity was very high.

The lynchpin of the successful masterplan was the proposed clearance of Shambles Square Market Place, in turn providing a visual and physical connection between the medieval quarter of the city centre, anchored by the Cathedral and Chetham's School of Music to the north, and St Ann's Square to the south. Accordingly, on 1 April 1998 a planning application for a new pedestrian street that would deliver this vision was submitted to Manchester City Council. Like most other elements of the bomb-damaged core, it was considered by the council at breakneck pace and approved on 14 May 1998. Demolition of Shambles Square (in tandem with the relocation of the two Shambles pubs – see 'Historic' chapter) commenced in late 1998. On the 1 September 1999 New Cathedral Street was opened to members of the public – the first new street in Manchester city centre for 50 years.

The other component that has enhanced connectivity throughout the centre has been the development of the comprehensive commercial districts, significant residential growth and the enhanced leisure and retail offer. What this means is that people now have a reason to walk around the city centre – from east to west and north to south. In terms of activity at the ground level, the city council has also placed a strong emphasis on developers providing 'active frontages' – in others, retail units ready for potential tenants. In the years before the bomb, many streets in Manchester, including the northern element of the Arndale Centre, were marked by blank walls, limited pedestrian activity and a fear of crime. People, therefore, would avoid these streets, and they became 'no go' areas. Even though these new developments may contain spaces that have yet to be let, it will be advantageous in the long term as, once an operator is in place, there will be activity, footfall and a destination for shoppers.

▲ St Ann's Square and New Cathedral Street.

© Aidan O'Rourke – www.aidan.co.uk

▲ Cannon Street, March 2002.

© Euan Kellie

▲ Arndale Centre signage, Cannon Street.

◄ The inclusion of ground floor retail frontages in new developments.

© Euan Kellie

© Euan Kellie

WATERWAYS

Manchester city centre is blessed with several rivers and canals, all of which are assets and theoretically perfect for traffic-free walking. While great progress has been made in places, there is still much to do, and in line with this are priorities for improvement and enhancement. Inevitably, once these assets become hubs of activity the perceived problems of pedestrian safety and security will gradually disappear.

RIVERS

Irk

The Irk flows through the northern suburbs of Manchester outside the immediate city-centre boundary (in places such as Collyhurst) before merging with the River Irwell beneath Victoria railway station at Ducie Bridge.

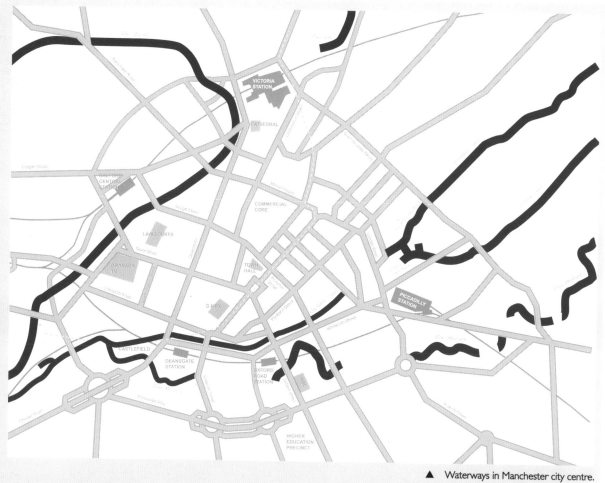

▲ Waterways in Manchester city centre.

Irwell

The Irwell is 39 miles (63km) in length, starts in Cliviger located in Burnley and twists and bends through to Salford. The three local authorities of Manchester City Council, Salford City Council and Trafford Metropolitan Borough Council, together with the Central Salford Urban Regeneration Company, are, as of 2010, in the process of promoting the 'Irwell City Park' project. Valued at £45 million, it seeks to enhance the River Irwell across six designated zones which stretch from Peel Park and the heart of Salford through to Salford Quays and the Lowry and Imperial War Museum.

Medlock

The Medlock starts in the hills surrounding Strinesdale to the east of Oldham and flows for 10 miles (16km), under the car park of the City of Manchester stadium and into the heart of the city centre by Potato Wharf and Castlefield. The river has been identified by Manchester City Council as integral to the delivery of new city-centre communities in New East Manchester.

Town Centre Securities

◀ Rochdale Canal following restoration work, Piccadilly basin.

CANALS

Ashton

The Ashton Canal Corridor begins in Ancoats, starting at Great Ancoats Street. New developments have contributed to the improvement of the Canal, particularly the New Islington Eco Park which links the Ashton and Rochdale Canal and the Islington Wharf development.

Bridgewater

At 39 miles in length, the Bridgewater forms the strategic link between the North and South canal network stretching from Runcorn to Leigh. At its peak, the canal carried more than 3 million tonnes of traffic. Today it forms part of the popular boat cruising route known as 'The Cheshire Ring', passing through Manchester city centre where it joins up with the Rochdale Canal.

Rochdale

The canal runs for 32 miles (50km) across the Pennines from the Bridgewater Canal at Castlefield Basin in Manchester to join the Calder and Hebble Navigation at Sowerby Bridge in West Yorkshire. An interesting walking route along the canal is known as the 'Rochdale Nine', the flight of locks at the Manchester terminus of the trans-Pennine Rochdale Canal. It starts at Dale Street near Piccadilly Station, flows alongside Canal Street, Whitworth Street West and concludes at the confluence with the Bridgewater Canal in Castlefield.

PROVISION OF PUBLIC OPEN SPACE

Open space in the city centre has taken a variety of forms over the years – hard, traditionally paved areas, and soft, grassed areas with additional planting. There is a very important point to make in telling the story about such provision in the city centre – its use. Rather than simply providing large expanses of hard or soft open space, the key has been to introduce areas that people want to use – not something that is simply incidental. Following the bomb, several key pieces of open space have been introduced (and in some cases enhanced) in the city centre.

▼ Cathedral Gardens.

CATHEDRAL GARDENS

The gardens sit in the designated Millennium Quarter area of the bomb masterplan and are bound by the approach to Victoria Station, Chetham's, the Cathedral and the Triangle. The quarter was one of many places across the country where a project would be delivered by the Millennium Commission (a short-life, independent organisation set up in 1993 by the National Lottery Act). As outlined on the Millennium Commission website:

'The Millennium Commission assisted communities in marking the close of the second millennium and celebrating the start of the third. The Commission used money raised by the National Lottery to encourage projects throughout the nation which enjoyed public support and would be lasting monuments to the achievements and aspirations of the people of the United Kingdom.'

© Euan Kellie

REBUILDING **MANCHESTER**

▶ Cathedral Gardens and Urbis.

© Aidan O'Rourke - www.aidan.co.uk

It was an important and sensitive piece of land located in the heart of the Cathedral conservation area and surrounded by listed buildings. By the time of the bomb it had been in operation as a temporary surface car park for over a decade. Several planning permissions had been granted following the clearance of the buildings on Fennel Street and Long Millgate in the late 1980s, including consent (twice) for a hotel in both 1981 and 1984. By the time of the bomb these visions had not been delivered.

There was a need to introduce public open space which would respond to its surroundings, namely: the Cathedral, Urbis, Corn Exchange and Chetham's School of Music. BDP, who had been beaten into second place in the masterplan design competition by Edaw, were selected in 1998 to design a £4.4 million 'city park'. In an interview with *Landscape Review* in October 2002, BDP Landscape Director Karen Howell outlined the vision:

'We went for contrast. We wanted something totally different from Exchange Square, and to bring the park concept back into the city. This lead us to a design that included large expanses of rolling lawns, plenty of trees and a water feature.'

The gardens, which opened to the public in July 2002, represented Manchester's first city-centre park for 70 years. It has gone on to secure a series of awards including The Civic Trust Special Award for Urban Design 2004, Environment Award 2002 and Manchester Civic Society Award 2002.

EXCHANGE SQUARE

As touched on earlier in this chapter, the provision of space outside the Corn Exchange and along Hanging Ditch had been a priority for the city council for many years, particularly post-war. One of the priorities within Edaw's masterplan was to enhance the area further, particularly with the provision of the new Marks & Spencer building, the closure of Cannon Street (which provided an east-west pedestrian route although people would generally try and avoid it) and relaxed traffic flows along Corporation Street (and the improved Arndale Centre).

In seeking a 'signature' piece of open space that would counteract the soft space of Cathedral Gardens (or City Park, as it was known at the time, behind the Corn Exchange) a design competition was held for what would be known as 'Exchange Square'. Four entries were submitted by various practices. Manchester Millennium and Manchester City Council had high expectations for the area, and the chosen design solution had to be the very best.

Having reviewed the entries, the panel was unconvinced. In an article published by the *Architects Journal News* on 15 October 1997, chairman of Manchester Millennium Sir Alan Cockshaw, who was head of the jury, outlined his thoughts:

'The four schemes offered water features, stone elements or ingenious level changes, but none gave us the totality of the solution we were looking for.'

It was at this point that Massachusetts-based Landscape Architects Martha Schwartz Partners were invited to submit a scheme for the square. They duly obliged. Their proposals sought to address the change in topographical levels by introducing a plaza immediately in front of the new Marks & Spencer building. The designs were warmly received by Manchester Millennium. An area of contention, however, was the proposed introduction of five ersatz palm trees, dotted across the square. Following discussions, the trees were removed from the scheme in early 1999 (announced by

▲ The Corn Exchange and Hanging Ditch in 1995 – a year before the bomb.

▲ Exchange Square.

◄▼ Exchange Square.

© Aidan O'Rourke - www.aidan.co.uk

the *Evening News* on 29 April with the headline 'fake trees are facing the axe') and replaced with four tilting steel windmills, a design by local artist John Hyatt.

Following completion of the square in November 1999, it has become a very popular location in Manchester. It is a dynamic location which benefits from the vibrancy of the surrounding uses. Further attractions have since been added. In May 2003 a TV screen was mounted on the side of The Triangle (providing a focal point) and in 2004 a 60m-high Ferris wheel with 42 carriages known as the Wheel of Manchester was introduced (still in place in 2010). Like other areas of open space in the city centre, it is now home to a series of markets offering food, drink and gifts during the Christmas period.

As specific uses surrounding the square, such as The Triangle, are enhanced over the coming years, along with the Medieval Quarter to the rear, it is probable that it will become an even more important destination in the city centre, attracting more and more visitors.

PICCADILLY GARDENS

Following the completion of these two pieces of new public open space in the bomb core, the hunger for regeneration moved eastwards towards the somewhat outstanding matter of Piccadilly Gardens. The 10-acre site also formed part of the masterplan for the bomb core (located within the 'outer ring') and had, without question, been a significant priority for the city council for many years. In stark contrast to its halcyon days in the 1950s and 1960s when it was the anchor of the city centre (mirrored by the proposals outlined in the 1945 Plan along with the Piccadilly Plaza development) by the late 1990s the gardens had lapsed into a state of disrepair and notoriety, marked by anti-social behaviour. Rather

▼ Piccadilly Gardens, 1999.

© Aidan O'Rourke - www.aidan.co.uk

than being a place to visit, it had become a place to avoid – not helped by the fact that it was sunk into the ground, marking the basement of the former Royal Infirmary.

It was vitally important that the gardens be radically improved – particularly in light of its 'gateway' location and close relationship with Piccadilly Station. In an article published by the *Estates Gazette* on 11 May 1999 Leader Richard Leese made it clear that the priority was to deliver an area which would have:

'a positive and welcoming first impression for visitors to Manchester who pass through the area when arriving in the city'.

Following the appointment of a design team – which included Edaw; engineers Arup; renowned Japanese architect Tadao Ando; local architects Chapman Robinson; and lighting engineer, Peter Fink – a scheme for the gardens was prepared and submitted to the city council for determination. In 1999 two proposals were put forward. The first was the refurbishment of the gardens (a detailed application). The second, which sought only outline permission, was for an office building which would take up a piece of land within the gardens, facing Portland Street. To fund the redevelopment of the gardens, the council would have to sell this piece of land, thus raising the necessary capital. The formula was simple: no office building, no gardens. People were not happy with the concept. The Planning Committee Report dated 30 September 1999 outlined the city's position:

'The situation here is quite simple in that the cost associated with the environmental works is high, in the region of £10 million, and while some funding will come from the private sector the remainder will be found from European sources and from matched public funding provided by the council. There are no grants available to the city council for such works (over and above European, ERDF funding) and the council's one option is to realise capital sums through the sale of assets. Put another way, without the council's contribution European funding is not available and no other action to improve the Gardens would be possible in the foreseeable future.'

Permission was granted by the Planning Committee. However, the journey was not over. A detailed proposal would be needed for the office building before anything else could happen. Akin to the Piccadilly Place story, the city council chose to work with developers Argent, who would be responsible for delivering this commercial element. The design of the building was the subject of an International Design Competition, which was won by architects Allies and Morrison.

The proposal, once submitted as a planning application in July 2000, would also generate much opposition and lead to a coalition of campaigners who fiercely sought to stop the proposed development. According to an article published by the *Evening News* on 21 September 2000 there were 10 separate applications to register the gardens as a 'Village Green' (this is a legal process where registration as a 'village green' would protect land and mean that any development could be a criminal offence). A further concern raised by objectors was the relocation of five statues surrounding the gardens: Watts, Queen Victoria, Wellington, Peel and Adrift. All were listed with the exception of Adrift, hence permission was needed for their relocation.

Despite the endeavours of the objectors the applications were approved by the city council in September 2000. The revitalised gardens would go on to be delivered in time for the Commonwealth Games, opening to the public in May 2002. The office building, One Piccadilly Gardens, was completed in early 2004 and offered six floors of office space, along with ground floor uses. Property consultants King Sturge were the first tenants in January 2005, followed in September by the Bank of New York who leased 91,000sq ft of office space (8,454m²) – one of the most important and high-profile lettings in the city during the decade. This provided further evidence that Manchester city centre was becoming a true business destination, attracting local, national and international businesses.

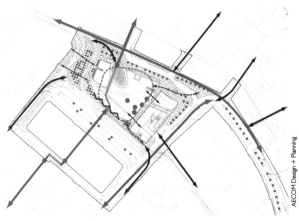

▲ Piccadilly Gardens, circulation routes.

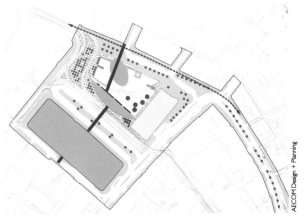

▲ Piccadilly Gardens, the layout of key elements including the elliptical fountain.

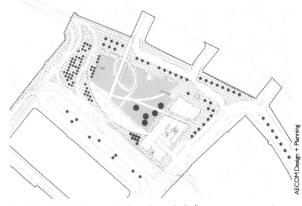

▲ Piccadilly Gardens, a planting scheme including numerous new trees.

© Euan Kellie

▲ One Piccadilly Gardens under construction, February 2002.

▶ Piccadilly Gardens.

AECOM Design + Planning

Argent Estates Limited

▶ One Piccadilly Gardens.

© Aidan O'Rourke - www.aidan.co.uk

▲   Piccadilly Gardens.

◄   Fountains, Piccadilly Gardens.

In tandem, and like many of the stories told in the 'Commercial' chapter, further investment was delivered in the immediate vicinity of the gardens. Bruntwood committed to the enhancement of Piccadilly Plaza (considered later in this chapter) along with a series of other office buildings along York Street (now known as New York Street) and Argent went on to deliver Piccadilly Place.

The gardens are, once again, an area of great importance and vibrancy, with estimates in 2008 indicating that 28 million people walk through them each year. As with most projects, elements of the completed scheme have attracted controversy. A 130m-long concrete wall on the perimeter of the gardens, designed by Tadao Ando, has not been to everyone's liking. Indeed, the level of opposition is such that a Facebook group called 'People who hate the concrete monstrosity in Piccadilly Gardens' has been set up! Thankfully, the group's opening page pays tribute to the rest of the gardens:

'By the way – what is hidden behind the wall is very nice indeed – several water jets and some lush green grass.'

Manchester City Council, Cityco and the Piccadilly Partnership have played a fundamental role in making this happen by promoting events to draw people into the gardens (such as 'Platform 4 Piccadilly', a music, theatre and dance event held in the gardens with contributions from a spectrum

▼   Piccadilly Gardens, 2003.

© Aidan O'Rourke - www.aidan.co.uk

of companies including Chol; Fittings; Marc Brew; stopGAP; Akademi; Kompany Malakhi and Kazzum). Similarly, they have been faced with the challenge of managing and maintaining the grassed areas – a direct result of the area becoming popular again!

GREAT NORTHERN SQUARE

On the flip side there has been the delivery of high-quality open space that, sadly, by 2010 has not yet managed to attract thousands of users on a regular basis.

Forming part of the Great Northern Initiative, architects Skidmore, Owings and Merrill identified the opportunity to create the square as an entrance to what would be Manchester's emerging business and hospitality district, incorporating not only the Warehouse but also the GMEX and International Conference Centre. The square, which was completed in 2001, consists of high-quality hard and soft landscape features, including a terraced amphitheatre at its centre. Restaurants and cafés, such as Bar 38, are provided to the north of the square.

While the design of the square is wonderful, it has yet to succeed as a destination in its own right. Hopefully in the future it, along with the Great Northern Warehouse, will host more events and become a place which attracts footfall and activity.

Tony Woof

▶ Great Northern Square.

SPINNINGFIELDS: HARDMAN SQUARE

Importantly, the provision of public open space – hard and soft – has been factored into Spinningfields from the outset, forming a critical piece of the masterplan supported by the city council. The public spaces have been used effectively with events such as 'Screenfields' – held in 2009 where a 16.5ft by 10ft screen located in Hardman Square screened the British Grand Prix, Wimbledon, The Ashes, Royal Ascot and the Johnnie Walker Championship at Gleneagles – and 'Spinningfields Ice Rink', also held in Hardman Boulevard, along with other attractions including a magical carousel ride and a temporary arctic bar, The North Pole.

As a marker of success, in 2008 Manchester was named by the Civic Trust (under their Green Flag Award scheme) as the lead authority in the country for the third year in a row, with 27 of its green spaces placed in the list of best parks in England and Wales. Notably, three of these spaces are located in the city centre: Parsonage Gardens, St John's Gardens and Sackville Gardens. The city centre is actually blessed with many elements of public open space, hard and soft, large and small. What is crucial to the success of such space, both today and in the future, is its functionality.

What is also apparent is the focus and priority given to public open space within forthcoming proposals and masterplans. With the growth of proposals that sought to provide tall buildings in the city centre, the city council saw an opportunity to put developers in a position where such proposals would be allowed on the basis that they 'gave something back' – in other words, by providing open space accessible to all. Many of the major initiatives within the city centre constructed during the first decade of the new millennium (such as Piccadilly Place, Piccadilly Basin and Spinningfields) have consequently been driven around not only height and design quality, but also the connectivity with the rest of the centre and the provision of public space with a use – places where events and attractions can be held, not simply a token gesture to secure a planning permission.

The city council's 'City Centre Strategy for 2009–2012' affirms the importance – and relevance – of high-quality public space and its contribution to the future economic prosperity of Manchester:

'The importance of investing in high-quality public spaces to create a truly magnificent public realm is also vital to underpinning the competitiveness of the retail offer.'

UPGRADED TRANSPORT INTERCHANGES

Manchester's major transport interchanges have also received considerable attention in the years following the bomb. In terms of improving the city's image this has been an important part – after all, first impressions count.

▲▼ 'Screenfields', Spinningfields.

▼ Public open space in Manchester city centre.

1	Angel Meadow
2	New Islington
3	Ardwick Green
4	Hulme Park
5	Catalan Square
6	Castlefield Arena
7	The Lowry Hotel piazza
8	Cathedral Gardens
9	Smithfield
10	Stevenson Square
11	Piccadilly Basin
12	Granby Row
13	Roman Gardens
14	St John's Gardens
15	Crown Square
16	Exchange Square
17	Piccadilly Gardens
18	Piccadilly Place
19	Sackville Gardens
20	Barbirolli Square
21	Great Northern Square
22	Hardman Square
23	'Motor Street Square'
24	Parsonage Gardens
25	St Ann's Square
26	Lincoln Square
27	Albert Square
28	Peace Gardens
29	St Peter's Square

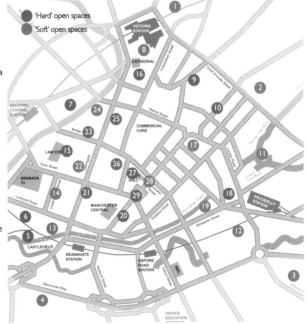

▲▶   Piccadilly Station, 1988.

PICCADILLY STATION

By the time of the bomb in June 1996, Piccadilly Station, which opened in 1842, had become a grim place to visit. No significant work had been undertaken at the station since the 1960s, and consequently it was looking tired and dated. With nearly 65,000 passengers using the station each day and with the Commonwealth Games on the horizon, it was vital that this crucial gateway to Manchester city centre be upgraded as soon as possible.

Like many other parts of the 'Piccadilly Gateway', improving the station was a priority for the city council. From the outset, and following initial feasibility studies undertaken during 1996, it became clear that the brief was to deliver a new station, fit to compete on the international stage: Piccadilly Station therefore had to provide an exceptional experience for all visitors. Initial work commenced between 1997 and 1999 with the refurbishment of the roof. With a comprehensive design team on board, including Building Design Partnership appointed as architects, a planning application was submitted in early 2000 for a new station frontage facing onto London Road, including the reworking of the internal space. As with many of the projects introduced already in the book the ethos of trust shared between the project team, the city council and, due to the presence of listed buildings, English Heritage, led to a prompt decision. The application was approved in July 2000, and construction work followed shortly after.

It became, at the time, the most significant new mainline station in the UK for almost 40 years. The project introduced new buildings, lifts, elevators and travelators, as well 31 shops and cafés (previously there were only 13). A multi-storey car park was introduced on Boad Street adjacent to the station, providing a physical connection by way of a road bridge to the existing car park at station level.

© Aidan O'Rourke - www.aidan.co.uk

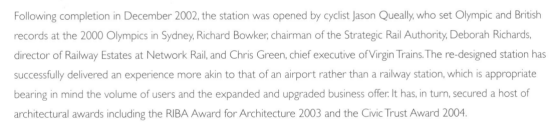

© Aidan O'Rourke - www.aidan.co.uk

▲ Entrance, Piccadilly Station.

◄ Inside Piccadilly Station.

Following completion in December 2002, the station was opened by cyclist Jason Queally, who set Olympic and British records at the 2000 Olympics in Sydney, Richard Bowker, chairman of the Strategic Rail Authority, Deborah Richards, director of Railway Estates at Network Rail, and Chris Green, chief executive of Virgin Trains. The re-designed station has successfully delivered an experience more akin to that of an airport rather than a railway station, which is appropriate bearing in mind the volume of users and the expanded and upgraded business offer. It has, in turn, secured a host of architectural awards including the RIBA Award for Architecture 2003 and the Civic Trust Award 2004.

SHUDEHILL TRANSPORT INTERCHANGE

One of the key objectives outlined by the Edaw masterplan and guidance for the bomb-damaged area was the provision of a transport interchange in the northern part of the city that would provide a multi-storey car park, a tram stop and a bus terminating facility – a direct replacement for the Arndale bus station devastated by the bomb. The chosen location for this development was on Shudehill, located between Victoria Station and the Northern Quarter.

The delivery of the interchange took longer than anticipated. According to an article published by the *Estates Gazette* on 28 January 1999, a number of parties had objected to the proposals during the planning process including the CIS – a division of Co-operative Wholesale Society – who owned the land adjacent to the bus station. This is a very clear, and

▶ Shudehill Transport Interchange.

▲▼ Shudehill Transport Interchange.

useful, example of what could go wrong if parties could not fundamentally agree with a proposal (much like the Free Trade Hall story in the 'Historic' chapter). While this project was relatively small when considered against other elements of the masterplan, it is an excellent example of how Manchester City Council and the task force successfully delivered the rest of the reconfigured city centre. Consider it another way: if such conflicts had existed with other landowners elsewhere in the bomb-damaged core, the rebuilding could have taken significantly longer.

In this instance, Ian Simpson Architects and Jefferson Sheard Architects went on to work together and prepare a design solution that was appropriate for the site. Planning permission was finally granted in March 2001, and construction finally commenced in 2003. The scheme was completed in early 2006 and delivered over 800 parking spaces.

In 2007, the completed building received a RIBA Regional Award and a RICS Innovation Award.

The Picc-Vic Project

In terms of transport connections, the story of the 'Picc-Vic' project is fascinating. It was a huge underground railway that appeared on the city council's 'action list' on several occasions during the 19th and 20th century. The story is told by Keith Warrender in his fascinating book *Underground Manchester: Secrets of the City Revealed.*

The concept first appeared in 1839 but was quickly vetoed by those with shares in the Ship Canal. The concept re-emerged in 1912 when it was announced that Manchester city centre would have its own 'tube railways'. Sadly, such grandiose aspirations were eliminated by way of World War One two years later. The revised scheme was driven around an inner city of stations and lines, branching off to five districts. In an attempt to convince sceptics, Councillor T. Walker, the Chair of the Underground Rail Committee, was willing to commit to the project:

'Manchester will start boring it's underground railway station this year – that is a declaration, I can make it with the utmost confidence.'

Sadly, he was over-confident. The Great Depression took hold and by 1933 the plans were, once again, obsolete.

The vision for an underground rail network reappeared with the announcement in 1972 of the 'Picc Vic' proposals. The scheme would include a 2.75-mile connection from Ardwick Junction to the Queen Road Junction on Bury Lane. Five central stations were announced, located across the city centre in a south-north direction: Piccadilly Low Level, Whitworth, Central, Royal Exchange Theatre and Victoria Low Level; however, as with all the previous iterations of the project, funding was a problem. Between 1973 and 1975 the government announced grant cuts and, consequently, the scheme was delayed. By 1977, despite considerable preparation work including the acquisition of property and construction sites along with underground tunnels and shafts, the £156 million scheme was, once again, officially abandoned.

Following the abandonment of the underground rail system in the 1970s, attention returned in the 1980s to the idea of light rail. The Metrolink followed shortly after in 1992. Not a bad compromise.

▲ The 'Picc-Vic' project.

Manchester City Council

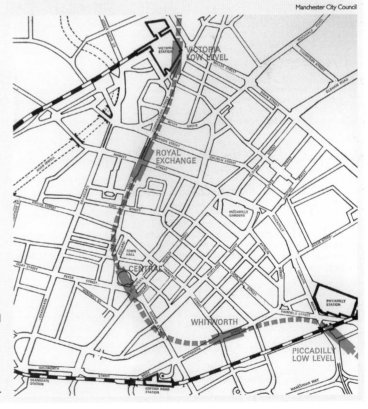

Manchester City Council

▶ 'Picc-Vic' tunnel alignment in Manchester city centre.

REBUILDING **MANCHESTER**

▲ Corporation Street in 1992. Marks & Spencer and Longridge House to the left, with the Arndale Centre to the right.

▲ Proposed pedestrian footbridge.

AESTHETIC IMPROVEMENTS

The final part of the space and connectivity story is that of aesthetic improvements to, what were at the time, two of Manchester city centre's most significant eyesores: The Arndale Centre and Piccadilly Plaza.

ARNDALE CENTRE

The book has already introduced the many improvements to the Arndale Centre following the bomb in 1996. Perhaps one of the most symbolic pieces of work related to the pedestrian footbridge across Corporation Street, which originally connected the Arndale Centre with Marks & Spencer and the Shambles Square Market Place development. The bridge, which had been approved by the city council in June 1976 and delivered shortly after, was symbolic of architecture in the 1960s and 1970s and the delivery of 'streets in the sky'.

▼ Corporation Street footbridge.

On Saturday 15 June 1996 the truck bomb was parked underneath the bridge and was unsurprisingly decimated by the blast. The shattered structure was removed four days after the bomb and was one of the first pieces of the city centre to be demolished.

Once the decision had been made by the task force and city council, in conjunction with the various landowners, to keep the bridge rather than remove it, the priority was high-quality design. Like the rest of the bomb core, it would be appropriate to replace the bridge with something contemporary and eye catching rather than simply putting the old one back. A design competition was held by the task force, which was won by architects Hodder Associates in December 1997.

Following design review and ongoing discussions with the city council (in particular, the highways department) and Manchester Millennium, a planning application was submitted and then approved in October 1998. It was constructed throughout 1999 and was opened to the public, with the new Marks & Spencer, on 25 November 1999.

Hodder + Partners

▲ Corporation Street footbridge.

Here are some interesting facts:

- The span of the bridge is 20m and is skewed appropriately four degrees.
- There is a vertical clearance of 6m above Corporation Street.
- It is made up of a structural net of steel longitudinal tensions rods and associated hoops.
- There is a difference in site and floor levels: the bridge slopes upward from Marks & Spencer to the Arndale at a gradient of 1:14.5.
- There are two level landings at end of the bridge, which ensures that it can 'sit' between the buildings.

The design quality of the bridge has since been recognised with two awards: the Structural Steel Award and a RIBA award, both of which were granted in 2000.

PICCADILLY PLAZA AND 'NEW' YORK STREET

The Piccadilly Plaza complex adjacent to Piccadilly Gardens was for many years nothing short of an eyesore. During the 1980s and 1990s it had become an isolated part of the Manchester city centre; a place that pedestrians would, quite rightly, avoid at all costs. Designed by architects Covell Matthews and constructed between 1960 and 1964, the complex consisted of a two-storey 'podium', along with two towers (Jarvis Piccadilly Hotel and the 29-storey Sunley Tower) and a pavilion building (Bernard House).

▲ Piccadilly Plaza in 1998 before refurbishment. Bernard House is visible on the right.

▼ Piccadilly Plaza.

In 1999, as part of the Piccadilly Gateway vision, previous owners Piccadilly Plaza Partnership introduced their plans for the complex which would include the refurbishment of the Sunley Tower offices (to be renamed City Tower), improvements to the existing Jarvis Hotel, a new shopping arcade to link Manchester's Northern Quarter and Chinatown, and improvements to the surrounding streetscape. A key piece of the redesign was the demolition of Bernard House, located at the corner of Mosley Street and Parker Street. Following receipt of planning consent for a comprehensive redevelopment of the Plaza in 1999, the building was demolished. As outlined in a paper prepared by Mr G. Sellers of Babtie, it was quite an experience:

'Going into this office was like going back 35 years! It was almost as if the clerk of works had slipped out for a site inspection. The 1950s desk, chair, cupboard, drawing board, plan chests, old fashioned telephone and adding machine they were all there, time warped in place.'

By March 2001 Bernard House had been demolished and the proposals, designed by Leslie Jones Architects, followed shortly after with the construction of a new building and aesthetic work to the ground and first-floor podium block.

As Piccadilly Gateway gathered momentum, particularly with completion of the new Piccadilly Gardens, developers Bruntwood acquired the plaza from Piccadilly Plaza Partnership in late 2003. Speaking to the *Estates Gazette* in an interview published on 13 December 2003, chief executive Chris Oglesby outlined the vision:

'This marks a new beginning for Piccadilly Plaza, fully integrating it into the regenerated Piccadilly Gardens. Piccadilly Plaza is a well-designed building which has suffered years of neglect. We have a team in place that will work closely with the city's planners, to deliver a scheme that will significantly enhance Manchester's skyline. We will ensure that the building never deteriorates to its current state.'

It was an entrepreneurial investment, capturing once again the Manchester attitude of making the best of existing assets. In 2004 it went on to be voted the Property Deal of the Year by *Insider Business Magazine*.

The next stage of the redesign was announced in the same year, prepared by architects Stephenson Bell. The Plaza would be split into three distinct components: the mall, which would offer a pedestrian route from Piccadilly Gardens through to York Street and China Town; an enhanced 'podium' with a series of new retail-facing refurbished office buildings along the re-titled 'New' York Street, Portland Street, Mosley Street and Parker Street; and a redesigned City Tower.

The revitalised scheme was a major improvement and would go on to win a commendation at the 2008 Manchester Society of Architects awards.

CONCLUSION

Space and connectivity in Manchester city centre has improved dramatically in the years following the bomb. It is easier (and more desirable) to navigate the city centre on foot; new, exciting, dynamic public open spaces have been introduced, while existing spaces have been enhanced; it is now a pleasure to use Piccadilly Station; and some landmark buildings that were eyesores have been transformed.

The message is as simple as this: the creation of a world-class city is far more than simply providing a collection of inspirational new buildings – the city must be as 'walkable' as possible. There must be links with the streets and waterways, making it an enjoyable experience.

There are challenges ahead. The management and maintenance of these spaces – and the creation of new streets and linkages – will be a priority. So, too, will be the upgrading of certain parts of the city centre (Stevenson Square in the Northern Quarter is a case-in-point). The waterways will also play a critical role. The Irwell City Park is an extremely exciting project which will unlock this potential and create a new strategic link with Manchester, Salford and Trafford.

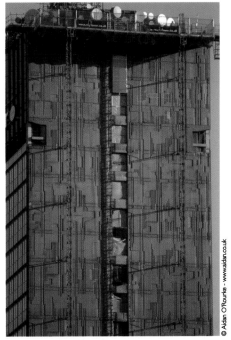

▲ City Tower prior to refurbishment.

▼ City Tower following external alterations.

'When it comes to the future you can let it happen and then wonder what happened, or you make it happen. Manchester has decided to make its own future in the world'.

– Financial Times

THE FUTURE

SO, WHAT NEXT?

To say the least, the future is very exciting. In 2010 a number of ambitious, forward-looking projects are in the pipeline – all of which will, in time, enhance and extend Manchester city centre, providing greater links and overlap with surrounding districts and the region.

The strengthened connection with Salford to the west will be particularly fascinating as it unfolds. While the Chapel Street 'quarter' lies within the administrative boundary of Salford City Council, the future for both cities includes a strong, shared strategic vision. A partnership approach between Manchester and Salford City Councils, together with key landowners, will help to bring about the comprehensive redevelopment of this wider area and create close linkages. This whole process is perhaps characterised by the River Irwell, which marks Manchester's immovable western boundary. Projects such as Irwell City Park (see 'Space and Connectivity') will bridge (literally) this physical divide and act as a vibrant link between the many different initiatives being developed along its banks.

This final chapter, therefore, considers two strands: the consolidation of the city centre, and the delivery of new comprehensive developments (both inside and outside the city-centre fringe).

THE CITY CENTRE

By continuing to champion high-quality design of new and refurbished buildings, along with the provision of exceptional public space, the city council will provide the conditions undoubtedly required to ensure Manchester is promoted as the destination of choice for investors, businesses, residents, shoppers and tourists, thereby sustaining the vitality and vibrancy of a leading, inspirational city centre.

© Euan Kellie

◀ Exchange Square.

REBUILDING **MANCHESTER**

▶ Central Salford project areas.

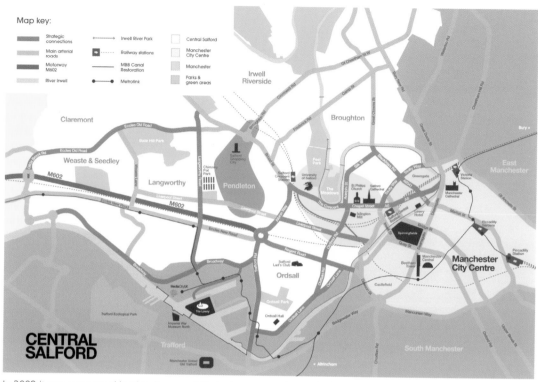

In 2009 it was announced by the city council that a five-year project, valued at £165 million, was to be launched. The scheme, titled the Town Hall Complex Transformation Programme, will create a new commercial location and upgrade and enhance some of the city's most important – and historic – buildings and spaces, including: the Town Hall, Town Hall Extension, Central Library and St Peter's Square (collectively known as the 'Civic Quarter'). This was, of course, a far cry from the visions outlined by Nicholas in the 1945 Plan. In February 2010 the first major piece of the development (promoted by Argent), the demolition of Elisabeth House and its replacement with an office building, 14 storeys high and designed by Glenn Howells Architects, was granted planning permission.

▼ St Peter's Square, 1996.

COMPOSITE PANORAMA OF ST PETERS SQUARE MANCHESTER © AIDAN O'ROURKE NOVEMBER 1996

◀ Visualisation of One St Peter's Square.

The city council will undoubtedly continue to encourage appropriate solutions for some of the most important historic buildings and spaces elsewhere in the city centre that need to be enhanced. This includes the area branded in the city council's '2009–2012 Strategic Plan' as 'Victoria' in the northern part of the city centre. Here, the objective is to create a new gateway destination with a modern and diverse retail and business offer, regional leisure facilities, and world-class public realm. The area contains Victoria Station, which in November 2009 was identified in a report by former Virgin Trains chief executive Chris Green and Town and Country Planning Association president Sir Peter Hall as top of a list of stations that have been 'left behind'. According to an article published by the BBC website on 17 November 2009, only 32 per cent of people using Victoria were happy with it.

The transfer of the Football Museum from Preston North End's football ground, Deepdale, to Urbis will also, without doubt, strengthen the role of the building while making a major contribution to the city's tourism portfolio. Similarly, the redevelopment of the Ramada complex (as presented at the end of the 'Residential' chapter), will also play a key role in delivering these objectives with almost 300,000sq ft (27,870m^2) of commercial space.

▼ Victoria Station.

REBUILDING **MANCHESTER**

▶ Fire Station, London Road.

© Aidan O'Rourke - www.aidan.co.uk

© Euan Kellie

▲ Future retail units, Spinningfields.

Equally important will be the enhancement of the former Fire Station on London Road. The building was designed by architects Woodhouse, Willoughby and Langham, opened in 1906 and is Grade II* listed. It closed in 1986 and, suffice to say, has been a priority on the city council's action list for many years.

Elsewhere, the continued success of retail in Manchester will depend on its diversity as well as its attractiveness as a place to visit and to walk around. The introduction of shops at Spinningfields such as Armani and Brooks Brothers will be particularly exciting as steadily new destinations, in addition to the Arndale Centre and Market Street, begin to appear. This whole experience will be underpinned by the quality of public open space and public realm. There are still some critical areas within the city centre that need to be improved, including not least of all Stevenson Square in the Northern Quarter. The importance – and potential – of this area is perhaps demonstrated by the commercial building known as 'The Hive'. Designed by architects HKR and branded by developers Argent Group as 'loft offices', the building is located on Lever Street and is due for completion in 2010. The scheme, which develops a site previously occupied by the Lever Street bus station, shows investor recognition that, with improved public realm and greater linkages, it can become a vibrant area, integrated with the rest of the city.

▲   Visualisation of 'The Hive', Lever Street.

© The Neighbourhood

▼   Unfinished Sarah Tower, Dale Street.   ▼   Sarah Village, Great Ancoats Street.   ▼   Unfinished building, River Street.

© Euan Kellie

© Euan Kellie

© Euan Kellie

REBUILDING **MANCHESTER**

▶ Future expansion of Manchester city centre.

Under the same heading, the revitalisation of Castlefield is also a priority. It needs to be closely integrated with surrounding areas, such as Southern Gateway and Hulme, and become once again a place where people want to be. Allied with this is the need to address schemes approved by the city council where construction has started – then stopped. Some of the decaying, incomplete eyesores include the Sarah Village development along Great Ancoats Street, Issa Quay and Sarah Tower on Dale Street and the development on River Street.

COMPREHENSIVE DEVELOPMENT PROJECTS

The various comprehensive development projects fall within two distinct categories: those located within the Inner Relief Route, and those that fall just outside. What is noticeable is that many of these projects are likely to provide a mix of uses, anchored by commercial development – an indication perhaps of Manchester's aim to consolidate its position as the main centre for financial and professional services in the UK, outside London. This continued growth can be best facilitated by the city council encouraging the provision of new commercial developments that, in turn, encourage investment by local, national and international businesses.

INSIDE THE INNER RELIEF ROUTE

A potentially major yet very exciting project that will continue the trend of re-using the former inner-city industrial heartland is that of the Mayfield Development proposals which will see the redevelopment of the former Mayfield Goods Yard, located to the east of Piccadilly Station (within the 'Eastern Gateway' quarter outlined in the City Centre Strategic Plan 2009–2012). The vision is to extend the city centre eastwards, creating a new mixed-use urban quarter for the co-location of around 5,000 civil servants drawn from the South East and parts of Greater Manchester. This will, without doubt, deliver a major piece of investment for Manchester city centre and the region. The 'Regeneration Framework for Mayfield', published in November 2009, outlined the objective:

▲ Derelict Mayfield Station.

'For central Government, Mayfield will contain a pioneering sustainable office campus aimed at setting new standards for the Civil Service estate, facilitating a major local and national relocation programme and delivering significant operational benefits.'

Crucially, the scheme will provide physical integration between the existing city centre and adjacent areas outside the Inner Relief Route; in particular, New East Manchester, and other neighbouring initiatives such as New Islington, the Ashton Canal Corridor, Ashton Old Road South and Ardwick. At the time of writing, the Eastern Gateway has, for many years, been characterised by a poor-quality environment comprising vacant warehouses, storage and distributions businesses, and poor linkages both within the area and with surrounding areas.

To the south the continued delivery of the Southern Gateway will be a priority. This portion of the city is particularly well placed to accommodate a significant growth in commercial activity given its relationship to 'The Corridor', Manchester's Universities and the Central Manchester Hospitals. Hence; the various component sub-areas which include First Street, the Great Jackson Street Framework Area, Macintosh Village and Oxford Road will also be of considerable interest, creating links across the city both east-west and north-south. Expanding the active heart of the city centre beyond the railway viaduct and connecting the city's economic base with Hulme, Hulme Park, Moss Side and Castlefield will be vitally important. Fantastic pieces of architecture such as Parkway Gate development by Ian Simpson Architects on Wilmot Street will play a role in delivering the vision.

▲ Parkway Gate, designed by Ian Simpson Architects.

▼ Visualisation of Greengate proposals.

In terms of the partnership approach with Salford City Council, key pieces of the jigsaw include the Greengate Embankment proposals located on the site of the old Exchange Railway Station in Salford. The first phase is already in place by way of the Abito apartment scheme completed in 2007, along with the adjacent residential development on Blackfriars Road known as Spectrum, delivered by developers Dandara. It will, in time, provide a new place for offices and business in the city centre and include significant new public spaces. As outlined by the Central Salford Urban Regeneration Corporation:

'Bounded by Chapel Street, Gravel Lane and Sacred Trinity Church and a stone's throw from Manchester Cathedral, this is a key site in the city's regeneration. The transformation of 13 hectares of vacant and derelict land will reconnect the historic centre of Salford to Manchester.'

Image by Visualisation One

OUTSIDE THE INNER RELIEF ROUTE

There are a variety of exciting projects and visions that will, in time, become new areas within a much larger Manchester city centre.

The redevelopment and regeneration of the Co-operative Group's existing 20-acre site (the Co-operative Complex) could provide a major office-led, mixed-use development at the northern gateway to the city centre. The Group's estate is bounded by Miller Street, Dantzic Street and Corporation Street. In September 2009 the anchor to the scheme, the Group's new headquarters, secured planning permission. Designed by architects 3D Reid, the scheme will provide 320,000sq ft (29,728m²) of open-plan office space over 15 storeys.

Within close proximity to the Green Quarter, the redevelopment of the former Boddingtons Brewery site will also be one to watch, with great potential to stimulate investment across the wider surrounding northern city fringe area. On the other side of the Green Quarter and the Co-operative complex are the plans for the Oldham Road and Rochdale Road corridors. This area forms part of the Strategic Regeneration Framework for North Manchester and is also a gateway area. By 2010 key developments include Skyline Central by West Properties, with other proposals such as 'Project Sharp' on Sharp Street – also by West Properties – in the pipeline.

In Salford, the redevelopment of Chapel Street comprises a major mixed-use scheme spanning 18 hectares, extending westwards towards the University of Salford. This development will ultimately create a link between the university and Manchester city centre. The scheme, which includes 849 new homes, 390 hotel rooms, 258,000sq ft (24,000m²) of retail, food, drink and entertainment space, and 2.1 million sq ft (197,000m²) of office space, was recommended for approval in February 2010.

While, as outlined at the beginning of the chapter, the majority of the schemes are commercially-led, there is also a focus on the expanding city-centre population (indeed, the majority of these schemes are likely to include a residential element). Estimates suggest that by 2012 the city-centre population will be 25,000. To ensure

◀ 'Project Sharp', Sharp Street

continued diversity in the population beyond this time, there is a need to attract families to the expanded city centre. This can only be achieved with the provision of necessary community infrastructure such as, among other things, health facilities and schools. This is, in truth, only likely to be possible in the inner areas beyond the city centre. Innovative projects such as New Islington, along with Ancoats Urban Village, will over the course of time play a leading role in satisfying this need. They will, like other projects, provide links with the city centre, the city-centre fringe, and beyond the fringe in places such as Miles Platting and Collyhurst.

▲ The Co-operative Group's new head office building, designed by architects 3D Reid. It is due for completion in 2012.

REBUILDING **MANCHESTER**

Will Alsop

▲　Visualisation of New Islington.

NEW ISLINGTON

The 13-hectare site is one of the seven Millennium Communities that have been promoted by the Homes and Communities Agency. It is being radically transformed by Urban Splash to an ambitious strategic vision by Will Alsop.

A new canal and water park, over 1,700 new homes, office space, a school, a health clinic, shops, bars and restaurants are planned. The site includes some wonderful pieces of contemporary architecture, most notably the 'Chips' building, also designed by Will Alsop.

◀　'Chips', New Islington.

▲　Royal Mills, Ancoats Urban Village.

ANCOATS URBAN VILLAGE

Ancoats Urban Village lies just to the east of Manchester city centre, covering an area of 20ha between the Rochdale Canal and Oldham Road. The long-term aim of the project, also part of 'New East Manchester', is to restore and enhance some of the wonderful former mills and other historic buildings while creating a new urban village of around 3,000 people with places to work and visit as well as to live.

By 2010 several projects had been delivered. 'Waulk Mill' at 51 Bengal Street had been converted into self-contained office accommodation by Urban Splash. The 'MM2' scheme at the junction of Great Ancoats Street and Jersey Street, a joint venture between Gleeson and Persimmon Homes, created retail and commercial space, together with 92 apartments and live/work units.

Progress had also been made with the 'Royal Mills' and 'Murray Mills' complex on Jersey Street, providing commercial and residential space.

▼　Ancoats Urban Village, Great Ancoats Street.

MANCHESTER 2045 A.D.

▲ Visualisation of Manchester city centre in 2045 – taken from the City of Manchester Plan 1945.

FINAL THOUGHTS

Rebuilding Manchester was inspired by the city's energetic response to the bomb detonated on 15 June 1996. Fourteen years on, this traumatic event, and the creative reaction to it, can be seen as part of the much bigger picture that is the reinstatement of Manchester as a vibrant, inspirational city, firmly placed within Europe's elite. What has been clear throughout this book is that the 'rebuilding' is more than just bricks and mortar. It is about **people**. It is about the ability and commitment of individuals in the city's public and private sectors to work together towards the shared goal of re-creating Manchester.

But this must be done pragmatically. It is impossible to plan too far ahead. Life is unpredictable. Look at Roland Nicholas' vision for Manchester in 2045, drafted in 1945 (shown opposite.) Very few of his predictions came to fruition. The bomb in 1996 was an unforeseen event that no one could have anticipated; however, it was the spirit of Manchester, its people, the relationships and the shared objectives that delivered the solution. Indeed, it is this framework that will ensure Manchester comes through the recent global economic meltdown, and subsequent recession, stronger than before.

So, with this in mind, it is time to draw this book to a close and ask some very simple questions: Why is there still a hunger for more? Why is it desirable to have more buildings and spaces? Why is there a need to expand the city centre? Can the city council not just sit back and say, 'that's it, all done. The city is complete'?

It is simple. In the future there will continue to be people who, like today, will make decisions and choices based upon basic human needs: where to live, work and have fun. Therefore, Manchester must continue to be 'ahead of the game' and be the place that people **choose** by harnessing the energy and creativity with which it is associated. It must continue to be the place that encourages and fosters innovation and new ideas. And it will.

After all, to quote Anthony H. Wilson: 'this is Manchester. We do things differently here.'